THE WESLEYA...

The Trinity

Samuel M. Powell

THE FOUNDRY
PUBLISHING

Copyright © 2020 by Samuel M. Powell
The Foundry Publishing
PO Box 419527
Kansas City, MO 64141
thefoundrypublishing.com

978-0-8341-3841-4

Printed in the
United States of America

All rights reserved. No part of this publication may be reproduced, stored in a retrieval system, or transmitted in any form or by any means—for example, electronic, photocopy, recording—without the prior written permission of the publisher. The only exception is brief quotations in printed reviews.

Cover design: Arthur Cherry
Interior design: Sharon Page

Library of Congress Cataloging-in-Publication Data
A complete catalog record for this book is available from the Library of Congress.

All Scripture quotations, unless indicated, are taken from THE HOLY BIBLE, NEW INTERNATIONAL VERSION®, NIV® Copyright © 1973, 1978, 1984, 2011 by Biblica, Inc.® Used by permission. All rights reserved worldwide.

Scripture quotations marked (NRSV) are taken from the New Revised Standard Version Bible, copyright © 1989 the Division of Christian Education of the National Council of the Churches of Christ in the United States of America. Used by permission. All rights reserved.

Scripture quotations marked (RSV) are taken from the Revised Standard Version of the Bible, copyright © 1946, 1952, and 1971 the Division of Christian Education of the National Council of the Churches of Christ in the United States of America. Used by permission. All rights reserved.

The internet addresses, email addresses, and phone numbers in this book are accurate at the time of publication. They are provided as a resource. The Foundry Publishing does not endorse them or vouch for their content or permanence.

10 9 8 7 6 5 4 3 2 1

For
*Terrie, Jason, Megan, Matthew,
Andrew, Audrey, and Juliette*

Contents

Acknowledgments	**7**
1. The Doctrinal Importance of the Trinity	9
Part I: The Trinity in the Economy of Salvation	**17**
2. Beginning with Salvation	19
3. The Trinity and Divine Revelation	22
4. The Trinity and Creation	34
5. The Trinity and Salvation	43
6. The Trinity and the Church	61
7. The Trinity and Worship	70
8. The Trinity and the Church's Holiness	79
9. The Trinity and the Spiritual Gifts	88
10. The Trinity and the Church's Mission	98
11. New Testament Eschatology	105
Part II: The Historical Development of the Doctrine of the Trinity	**117**
12. Trinitarian Theology before the Council of Nicea	119
13. The Council of Nicea	131
14. Post-Nicene Developments in Christology	140
15. Post-Nicene Developments in the Trinity and Pneumatology	148
16. Wesleyan Trinitarian Theology	156
Part III: Thinking about the Trinity Today	**159**
17. Continuing Trinitarian Controversies	161
18. Some Continuing Perplexities about the Trinity	173
19. Knowing the Trinity	179
Suggestions for Further Reading	**189**
Glossary	**190**

Acknowledgments

Thanks are due to my friends Bonnie Perry, Alex Varughese, and Al Truesdale for help in producing this book. Thanks go as well to my colleagues at Point Loma Nazarene University for their help over the years.

ONE

The Doctrinal Importance of the Trinity

Sooner or later each of us receives something that we are told is valuable—a gift, an heirloom, or whatever. Sometimes its value is evident, its usefulness clear—gifts of cash, for instance. At other times, with other gifts, we invoke the saying, "It's the thought that counts," knowing that, regardless of its purported value, we have no use for it. In these cases the only important consideration becomes the question of where we will store it, certain that occasionally it will be necessary to put the gift on display. It's not that we don't appreciate these sorts of gifts, but they occupy space, are often not to our taste, and perform no useful service.

For many Christians, the doctrine of the Trinity is such a gift. We have received it and have been told it is valuable. We feel obliged to keep it in a safe place and to display it on appropriate occasions. We even become indignant if anyone criticizes it. But many Christians wonder why it is valuable, what it is good for, or even what the doctrine actually is. So we dutifully store it away in a safe place and, when asked, bring it out to display our orthodoxy. However, like most extravagant gifts, it makes little difference to our daily existence.

The purpose of this book is to help Christians better understand the doctrine of the Trinity, and why it is so central to our faith, to discipleship, and to the Christian mission.

Why Is the Doctrine of the Trinity Important?

For one thing, the Trinity is the central Christian teaching about God. It distinguishes Christianity from Islam, from Judaism, and from other religions. It also distinguishes mainstream, orthodox Christianity from movements on the Christian periphery, such as the Church of Jesus Christ of Latter-day Saints (the Mormons), the Watch Tower Bible and Tract Society of Pennsylvania (Jehovah's Witnesses), and certain types of Pentecostalism. It is thus the distinctive Christian doctrine *par excellence*. It was, moreover, the first major doctrinal issue in Christian history, the first that required councils and creeds.

Additionally, the doctrine of the Trinity is important because it occupies a central and organic place in Christian theology: doctrines about Jesus Christ, the Holy Spirit, and salvation make no sense without the Trinity. It is the doctrinal glue that binds other doctrines into a coherent unity.

Finally, we note that the statements of faith of the various churches in the Wesleyan tradition are all Trinitarian, with the doctrine of the Trinity typically constituting the first article of faith:

> There is but one living and true God, everlasting, without body or parts, of infinite power, wisdom, and goodness; the maker and preserver of all things, both visible and invisible. And in unity of this Godhead there are three persons, of one substance, power, and eternity—the Father, the Son, and the Holy Ghost.

—Article 1, "Of Faith in the Holy Trinity," Articles of Religion of the Methodist Church (used by both the United Methodist Church and the African Methodist Episcopal Church)

We believe in one eternally existent, infinite God, Sovereign Creator and Sustainer of the universe; that he only is God, holy in nature, attributes, and purpose. The God who is holy love and light is triune in essential being, revealed as Father, Son, and Holy Spirit.
—Article 1, "The Triune God," Articles of Faith of the Church of the Nazarene

We believe in the one living and true God, both holy and loving, eternal, unlimited in power, wisdom, and goodness, the Creator and Preserver of all things. Within this unity there are three persons of one essential nature, power, and eternity—the Father, the Son, and the Holy Spirit.
—Article 1, "Faith in the Holy Trinity," Articles of Religion of the Wesleyan Church

There is but one living and true God, the maker and preserver of all things. And in the unity of this Godhead there are three persons: the Father, the Son, and the Holy Spirit. These three are one in eternity, deity, and purpose; everlasting, of infinite power, wisdom, and goodness.
—Article 1, "The Holy Trinity," Articles of Religion of the Free Methodist Church

And Yet...

In spite of our formal declarations about the Trinity—our affirmations of admiration and loyalty—the importance of this doctrine is often not evident in our worship and daily lives. Seldom do we hear sermons that clarify the doctrine and emphasize its importance to Christian faith and life. Seldom do we hear prayers and benedictions that reflect Trinitarian doctrine. We often hear the Trinity invoked during baptismal liturgy and in the marriage pronouncement but seldom during the celebration of the Lord's Supper. As a result, it would not be an exaggeration to say that this cardinal doctrine of the Christian church remains disconnected from the proper practice of Christian discipleship for many Christians. It constitutes a legacy of whose value we are certain but whose usefulness we doubt.

Why is this? Why do we say that the doctrine of the Trinity is of capital importance yet treat it as a useless gift? The reasons lie in the way the doctrine has been presented in the church's education of clergy and laypeople.

The doctrine is often explained and defended on the basis of weak and unconvincing appeal to the Bible. As Christians, our instinct is to look to the Bible for our teachings, and that instinct is sound, but we should honestly acknowledge that the doctrine of the Trinity is not expressly set forth in the Bible. To be sure, the Bible bears witness to God's Trinitarian life, but the doctrine we profess is not explicitly presented in the Bible. Failure to recognize this fact can lead to a fruitless search for proof-texts that are, at best, embarrassing and can damage the church's credibility and doctrinal affirmations. For instance, interpreters have ransacked the Bible looking for verses that suggest a plurality of divine persons. These include Genesis 1:26 ("Let us make humankind in our image");[1] Genesis 18 and 19 (when three strangers visit Abraham); and Isaiah 6:8 ("Who will go for us?"). In a later chapter we will discuss the appropriate way to draw the doctrine of the Trinity from the Bible. For now, it is enough to avoid simplistic attempts to find the doctrine in particular biblical passages.

Even worse than the misleading appeals to Scripture are the poor analogies often employed to illustrate the Trin-

---

1. My translation.

ity. Many are familiar with the hit parade of absurd efforts, such as that the Trinity is like the three parts of an egg, or the three forms of water (ice, liquid, and steam). These metaphors fall short not *because* they are metaphors but because they equate God's unity with the unity of material stuff; in them the Trinitarian persons become mere parts. Not only do these metaphors fail to illustrate anything of importance, but they also do damage to the Christian faith by implying things about God that are highly misleading.

Sometimes, especially in textbooks of theology written before 1980, the Trinity is presented as a speculative theory about God's eternal being in a way that is far removed from the doctrine of salvation. A glance at the table of contents of older theological textbooks will show that the Trinity discussions typically appear in early chapters along with proofs of God's existence. The doctrine of salvation comes much later. This approach does serious damage to the doctrine of the Trinity by ripping it from its natural connection to salvation. As a result, the doctrine receives an overly abstract and speculative character that removes it from the practice of Christian life.

Our corporate worship also does not typically promote a good understanding of the Trinity. For example, prayer and benedictions should be offered to God the Father, in the name of the Son, and in the power of the Spirit. Unfortunately, we too easily destroy the Trinitarian structure of prayer by indiscriminately praying to Jesus or to the Holy Spirit, forgetting that prayer should be offered *to* the Father, in the *name* of Jesus, and in the *power* of the Spirit.

Admittedly, the doctrine, as a result of its historical development, comes loaded with technical and somewhat abstruse terminology—especially Greek terms such as *homoousios* ("of the same substance"). Technical terminology does not lend itself to easy exposition.

Finally, it has proven difficult for teachers of the Trinity to reconcile the notion that God is a Trinity of persons with the belief that God is a personal being—a person. How can God be *a* person if God is *three* persons? This sort of puzzle has led to much unedifying speculation about how number applies to God.

As a result of our failure to develop effective ways of presenting the Trinity, we find ourselves in the paradoxical situation of possessing a doctrine of undoubted truth and existential importance that we allow to sit idle and unused in favor of other doctrines that give us profound insight into the human condition and rich resources for living the Christian life.

A Preliminary Response

The root of our problem with the Trinity lies in a misunderstanding of revelation. Our failure to understand the idea of revelation directly results in a misapprehension of the doctrine of the Trinity.

We begin with the affirmation that the ultimate and unsurpassable revelation of God is Jesus Christ. We begin here because Jesus is the Word, the *logos*, of God (John 1:1–4). Whatever God says to humankind is found in Jesus Christ, either expressly or implicitly (Luke 24:25–27; John 5:39–47; Acts 10:43). Theology is the church's work of bearing witness to this revelation in forms suitable for teaching and preaching and in ways that will nurture the life of the church. Accordingly, the doctrine of the Trinity is the Christian community's attempt, with fallible, human words and concepts, to bear witness to God's revelation. It is the church's understanding of the God who comes to us in Jesus Christ. It is the church's verbalization of our encounter with God who reveals. It is thus a prayer, a human word offered up to God in the service of God.

The doctrine, consequently, is not:

- An incomprehensible mystery. Defining it as such is often simply an excuse for not engaging in the hard, intellectual task of thinking. God is not an impenetrable mystery; on the contrary, God is revealed. In revelation God has laid open God's life to us and made it plain. That is why, when Philip asked Jesus to show him the Father, Jesus answered that by seeing Jesus they had seen the Father (John 14:8-9). Theology is the task of thinking through this revelation, this event in which God's being is disclosed to us. However, while God has chosen to reveal Godself, thereby making it possible for us to know God, that doesn't mean we necessarily will fully understand everything God is.
- A numbers puzzle. Trying to understand the doctrine of the Trinity is not a game of figuring out how three can be one. Number measures finitude; the infinite God cannot be measured with or described by numbers.
- A philosophical theory imported into theology. The doctrine of the Trinity rests on God's revelation, not philosophy. However, philosophy presents us with powerful tools by which to think about God. It would be foolish for us to ignore these tools.
- A teaching about three beings. Whatever else the doctrine of the Trinity may be, it is not a doctrine about three beings. The orthodox belief that God is three Persons should never be interpreted to mean three separate and distinct beings.

Where Do We Go from Here?

This book is divided into three sections. Part I shows the connections between the Trinity and the rest of theology: creation, eschatology, and so on. It argues that there is a Trinitarian logic in every branch of Christian theology. In particular, the Christian doctrine of salvation makes sense only when we see it as the work of the triune God. Part II traces the historical development of the doctrine of the Trinity, especially during the early centuries of Christianity, when the doctrine's distinctive vocabulary arose and some of Christianity's most troublesome debates took place. Part III addresses some of the ongoing issues associated with understanding the doctrine today.

The Trinity in the Economy of Salvation

Part I

TWO

Beginning with Salvation

The question of where to begin is always crucial; the choice of beginning determines all that follows. Even the Trinity has its own order: Father, Son, Spirit. Where, then, does one begin to understand the doctrine of the Trinity?

As noted in chapter 1, the point of departure in traditional textbooks of theology is highly abstract. Textbooks historically began with philosophical proofs of God's existence, followed by the doctrines of the Trinity and creation. Only much later would most of them introduce the doctrines about Jesus Christ and the Holy Spirit, along with teachings about salvation and the church. The traditional approach presents the Trinity as an abstract truth, disconnected from salvation and the concreteness of the Christian life. It reduces faith to cognitive belief and loses the connection between Christian doctrine and ethics. It presents the doctrine of the Trinity as a speculative theory about God's eternal being—a theory with only the slimmest association with salvation.

In search of a more satisfactory beginning, we start with the crucial event of human history: the incarnation and its extension in the giving of the Holy Spirit. In the incarnation, God unites with humankind, thus establishing salvation. In giving the Spirit, God creates the church as the body of Christ, thus founding the community of salvation. The incarnation and the gift of the Spirit are the theological basis for the doctrine of the Trinity. Everything Christian theology has to say about God is governed by its understanding of these events.

The incarnation tells us that God's being is one of life, of movement, of passage. In the incarnation, God's life passes over into and identifies with what is not God. God identifies with and becomes humankind—but without ceasing to be God. In giving the Spirit, God's life continues its extension into finitude as God is united with the Christian community and becomes the Spirit that the community shares with Jesus Christ, its head.

The movement of God into the world has a beginning and an end. It comes forth from the Father, proceeds through the mediation of the Son, and comes to completion in the Spirit, who leads all things back to the Father. God the Father is thus the beginning of all things and also the end, the *telos* (goal) of all things, as these passages suggest:

- "There is but one God, the Father, from whom all things came" (1 Cor. 8:6).
- "Then the end will come, when he hands over the kingdom to God the Father . . . When he has done this, then the Son himself will be made subject to him who put everything under him, so that God may be all in all" (1 Cor. 15:24a, 28).

The beginning and end in God frames the world of human existence. But God does not merely *appear* in the world. God *unites* with us, becomes one of us without ceasing to be God. This union is the meaning of God's love, for love is essentially a matter of union. In love, what we love becomes an integral part of our being. What I love becomes incorporated into me. That is why the death of a loved one is devastating; in death we lose a part of our being—we are ripped apart, death leaving jagged edges and gaps that can never be filled. When we affirm with John 3:16 that God loved the world, or with 1 John 4:8 that God is love, we are saying that God is the one whose being and nature are to unite with what is other than God. In summary, in the incarnation and in giving the Spirit, God assumes human nature into God's own life. God unites God's own being with ours and invites us into fellowship.

The theological term we use to discuss God's entry into the world—the sending of the Son and the giving of the Spirit, and the resulting salvation—is "economy." This term is a translation of the Greek word *oikonomia* (oi-ko-no-mi-a), which appears several times in the New Testament (Eph. 1:10; 3:2, 9; Col. 1:25; 1 Tim. 1:4) to denote the work of God in salvation. The term originally referred to the management of a household and then came to mean administration or arrangement more generally. So, in theological discourse, we refer to the economy of salvation—the entire range of what God does to effect human salvation. The economy of salvation is thus the point of departure for the doctrine of the Trinity.

It is customary to speak of the economic Trinity, by which we mean the appearance of the Trinitarian God in human history. We thus distinguish the Trinity as it appears in history from the Trinitarian nature of God's eternal being. The latter is often referred to as the *ontological* Trinity or the *essential* Trinity.

THREE

The Trinity and Divine Revelation

The Importance of Revelation: The Hidden God

As noted in the previous chapter, the point of departure for understanding the Trinity is the economy of salvation—the revelation of God in history. It is now time to explore this connection more deeply. Consider these biblical affirmations:

- "The LORD has said that he would dwell in a dark cloud" (1 Kings 8:12b).
- "No one has ever seen God" (John 1:18a).
- God, "who lives in unapproachable light, whom no one has seen or can see" (1 Timothy 6:16b).

These sorts of texts bear witness to a pervasive theme in the Bible: God cannot be seen and is instead—apart from revelation—hidden from us. Whatever we know of God, then, rests on revelation. God is not like other beings, whom we can know through ordinary experience or study and research. Our knowledge of finite beings in the universe is accordingly within our grasp, our control. We decide whether to know them, and we determine how we will know them—either through casual experience, scientific methods, or some other way. But the Bible is clear that our knowledge of God does not lie within our control. God determines when and how God will be known.

Some biblical texts speak of humans seeing God. These include Exodus 33:17–34:5, where Moses sees God's back but not God's face; Exodus 24:9–11, where the elders of Israel see God; Isaiah 6:1, Isaiah's vision of God in the temple; and Ezekiel 1, in which the prophet sees God in a storm. But were these actually cases of humans visually seeing God? Thinking so would contradict Deuteronomy's adamant insistence that at Sinai Israel *heard* God but *saw* no form (see Deut. 4:11–15; 5:22–26). According to Deuteronomy we know God through divine speech—the word—and not through physical seeing. With Deuteronomy's emphasis in mind, let us revisit biblical accounts of visions.

Exodus 33:17–34:5. The text declares rather strongly that God's face cannot be seen; Moses sees only God's back (see 33:18–23). This narrative symbolizes the fact that our knowledge of God is always indirect and incomplete.

Isaiah 6:1 tells us that Isaiah saw God, but it says nothing about God's appearance except that God's robe filled the sanctuary.

Ezekiel 1. We get the most insight into visionary experience by looking closely at this text. There are two things to note. First, Ezekiel's vision occurs during a storm; he saw God in the storm. This tells us that visions of God happen in conjunction with mundane experiences. Ezekiel did not simply see God; he saw God in the storm; the storm was a revelation of God. Second, Ezekiel's vision of God is ineffable—it cannot be literally described. That is why the phrase "something like" occurs repeatedly in this passage: Ezekiel saw "something like gleaming amber" (v. 4, NRSV), "something like four living creatures" (v. 5, NRSV), "something like a dome" above the creatures (v. 22, NRSV), "something like a throne" and "something that seemed like a human form" (v. 26, NRSV), and "something that looked like fire" (v. 27, NRSV). Even the vision of God itself is presented indirectly: Ezekiel wrote of the "appearance of the likeness of the glory" of God (v. 28, NRSV).

What at first seems to be a contradiction turns out otherwise. God cannot be seen; on the contrary, apart from revelation, God is hidden from us. Even texts that speak of humans seeing God typically present such moments not as seeing God in any literal way. We conclude, then, that God cannot be known in any ordinary way. We do not control when and how we know God. If we know God, it can only be because God has become revealed.

What Is Revelation?

What, then, is revelation? The word "revelation" is the English translation of the Greek word *apokalupsis*, which means to uncover (*kalupto* is the Greek verb that means to cover and thus to conceal or to hide).

In the New Testament, various things are said to be matters of revelation:
- The gospel has been revealed—that is, disclosed—through the preaching of Jesus and the apostles (Rom. 16:25; Gal. 1:12; Eph. 3:3).
- Prophetic speech occurs when someone receives a revelation (1 Cor. 14:6, 26).
- Visionary experiences are revelatory (2 Cor. 12:1, 7; Rev. 1:1).
- Paul went to Jerusalem in response to a revelation (Gal. 2:2).
- Knowing God requires the spirit of wisdom and revelation (Eph. 1:17).

Additionally, revelation has an eschatological connotation—it is the final things that are revealed: judgment (Rom. 2:5), the children of God (Rom. 8:19), and Jesus Christ in his second coming (1 Cor. 1:7; 2 Thess. 1:7; and 1 Pet. 1:7, 13; 4:13).

However, visions, prophetic oracles, and the apostles' preaching are revelation in only a secondary sense because they bear witness to the primary and ultimate revelation, Jesus Christ. This assertion rests on the first chapter of John's Gospel, where Jesus Christ is identified as the Word of God. Jesus is not just *a* revelation; he is *the* Word of God, the ultimate form of God's declaration to humanity. In him the creative word of Genesis 1 and the prophetic words of the Old Testament find their common basis and fulfillment. In Jesus Christ God speaks fully and definitively. Accordingly, Jesus Christ is revelation in the full and proper sense of the word. Everything else we call revelation is such because of its relation to Jesus Christ.

If Jesus Christ is the true and fundamental meaning of revelation, then we must move beyond thinking of revelation as imparting facts or propositions. Revelation is more than an act of divine speech or a declaration. It is instead God's coming into the world to unite with humanity. Revelation, in its highest sense, is inseparable from incarnation.

Revelation is thus the presence of God. But God's presence is not like the presence of a table in a room or an idea in the mind. God's presence involves union; in Jesus Christ God becomes flesh and takes our humanity into God's being. This is the meaning of revelation. That is why, when in John's Gospel Philip asks Jesus to show him the Father, Jesus responds that whoever sees Jesus has seen the Father (John 14:8–9). The revelation of God cannot be separated from the union of the divine Word with human flesh in Jesus Christ. Jesus Christ, the incarnate Word, does not *bring* the revelation of God; the incarnate Word *is* the revelation of God.

If revelation is ultimately about God's act of uniting with humankind, then we can see why revelation cannot be about the communication of information. Information can be useful and even necessary, but information does not achieve union and redemption. The words of the prophets were thus *revelatory* but not *revelation*. In them God spoke, but the prophetic words did not create union between God and humans. God spoke, and humans heard, but only in the fullness of time did God become human and thus stand revealed. Consequently, we should think of revelatory moments prior to Jesus Christ as preliminary and anticipatory forms of revelation, whereas Jesus Christ—the union of God and humanity—is revelation in the strict and proper sense of the word. With this act of union—the incarnation of the Word—God's revelation is complete.

The connection between incarnation and revelation helps us understand the nature of God's revelation in the Old Testament. From a Christian perspective, such revelation, although genuine, is preliminary and anticipatory. In the Old Testament, God authentically addresses us and approaches us; however, the Old Testament does not fully reveal God. It cannot—because Jesus Christ is the full revelation of God. Jesus Christ is present in the Old Testament by way of anticipation; the Old Testament's faith and hope point toward the messianic age. It is also important to acknowledge that there could *be* no New Testament without the Old Testament. From its beginning days the Christian church has insisted that the two testaments stand together. But Christ's anticipatory presence in the Old Testament requires fulfillment in a bodily presence, hence the necessity of the incarnation.

The Trinitarian Structure of Revelation

God's revelatory act of communion with humankind is possible only because God is a Trinity—the communion of the Father, the Son, and the Spirit. If revelation were only the communication of information, it would not require a triune God; such communication would require only a being of intense and exclusive unity—the sort of God affirmed in Islam. But if revelation is ultimately an act of union, of establishing communion, of entering into human being, then, as the following discussion will show, the God who reveals must be a Trinity. The doctrine of the Trinity is the Christian community's attempt to express in words the Trinitarian life of God, who seeks and achieves communion with humankind. Divine revelation, therefore, has a Trinitarian structure.

The Revelation of God the Father

Revelation is the disclosure of the Trinitarian life of God; however, there is a special sense in which it is God the Father who is revealed. Consider these Johannine passages:

- "No one has ever seen God, but the one and only Son . . . has made him known" (John 1:18).
- "No one has seen the Father except the one who is from God; only he has seen the Father" (John 6:46).
- "I have revealed you to those whom you gave me out of the world" (John 17:6a).
- "We know also that the Son of God has come and has given us understanding, so that we may know him who is true" (1 John 5:20a).
- Additionally, there is Matthew 11:27b: "No one knows the Son except the Father, and no one knows the Father except the Son and those to whom the Son chooses to reveal him."

These texts show that the mission of the Son is to disclose the Father. They imply that, apart from the revealing activity of the Son, God the Father remains hidden.

But in what sense is the Father hidden? After all, the Bible tells us that God's existence can be known to some extent apart from the revelation of the Son. The heavens tell of God's glory (Ps. 19:1), and God's power and nature are seen in created things (Rom. 1:19–20). What, then, does it mean that, without the revelation of the Son, God the Father is hidden?

It means that the knowledge of God available *via* the created world is not the knowledge of God that leads to salvation; it is not grounded in God's revelatory act of creating redemptive communion with humankind. It is one thing to know God as Creator by meditating on the created world; it is quite another to know God as Savior through the revelation of the Son. Knowledge of God as Creator is available to everyone, which is why in theology we speak of "general revelation" and "natural theology"—terms that refer to the knowledge about God that anyone can perceive, experience, or deduce by simply observing the world around them. But knowledge of God as Savior is grounded in the work of the Son, who reveals God as Father and Redeemer.

The Revelation of God the Son

The New Testament gives us two basic metaphors for understanding the Son's revelation: Word and image.

The metaphor of Word rests on the opening verses of John's Gospel. These verses affirm that the Word of God is eternal and divine but also that this Word became flesh and appeared as Jesus Christ (John 1:14–18). Jesus Christ is the incarnation of the divine Word (John 1:1–5). As such, Jesus is God's address to us, God's self-declaration to humankind. It is important to note that this Word of God, this revelation, is not the communication of information or facts but is a human being. God's revelation is the birth, life, death, and resurrection of this human being, who is the *incarnate* Word. To repeat a point already made: revelation is communion, fellowship. Jesus Christ, this historical man, is the communion of God with humankind.

The metaphor of image finds its home elsewhere in the New Testament:

- "... Christ, who is the image [*eikon*] of God" (2 Cor. 4:4b).
- "... being in very nature [*morphe*] God" (Phil. 2:6a).
- "The Son is the image [*eikon*] of the invisible God, the firstborn over all creation" (Col. 1:15).
- "The Son is the radiance of God's glory and the exact representation [*karakter*] of his being" (Heb. 1:3a).

The metaphor of image says several things. For one, it affirms that Jesus Christ is the true and authentic image of God. This is the New Testament's commentary on Genesis 1:27, which speaks of God creating humankind in God's image. For New Testament writers, if we want to see the image of God, we must look to Jesus. Jesus is, therefore, the restoration of God's creation—a second, and perfect, image to replace the original image mentioned in Genesis 1 that is corrupted by sin. More pertinent to the idea of revelation, the metaphor of image says Jesus Christ is how we see God—hence, Jesus's words to Philip about seeing God the Father by seeing Jesus Christ (John 14:8–9). Just as when we look at a mirror we see the reflection of the object in the mirror, so we see the reflection of God the Father in the life, death, and resurrection of Jesus.

Jesus Christ is thus the revealer and the revelation (1) because he is the Word of God, incarnate in human flesh, and (2) because he is the unique and perfect image of God.

The Revelation of God the Holy Spirit

So far we have focused on the affirmation that Jesus Christ is revelation. Now we need to add that for revelation to be revelation it must be received. Even if revelation were merely communication, it would still have to be received, for speaking not joined to hearing does not constitute communication. But, since revelation is communion, it is all the more necessary for it to be received; as an act of union, communion cannot occur unilaterally, as an act of one party alone.

The reception of revelation—the actualization of God's communion with humankind—brings us to the role of the Holy Spirit. Since Jesus Christ is the union of God and humankind, it is important that this union becomes real, not only in Jesus Christ but also in humankind more generally. In Jesus Christ, the eternal Word of God is united with human nature; but when we receive the Holy Spirit, we too become united with God—hence the New Testament's teaching that we become adopted children of God (Rom. 8:14–17). This union with God through the Holy Spirit draws us into the fellowship that exists between the Father and the Son and actualizes in us the Son's revelation of the Father.

The Spirit actualizes our communion with God in the act of rebirth (John 3:3–8; Titus 3:5) and sanctification (2 Thess. 2:13; 1 Peter 1:2). Rebirth is the beginning of our communion with God; sanctification is its continuation and completion. Both terms signify our being brought into fellowship with God—our entering into the eternal fellowship between the Father and the Son in the power of the Spirit. As we enter the fellowship and dwell therein, we are united with God, and revelation is completed.

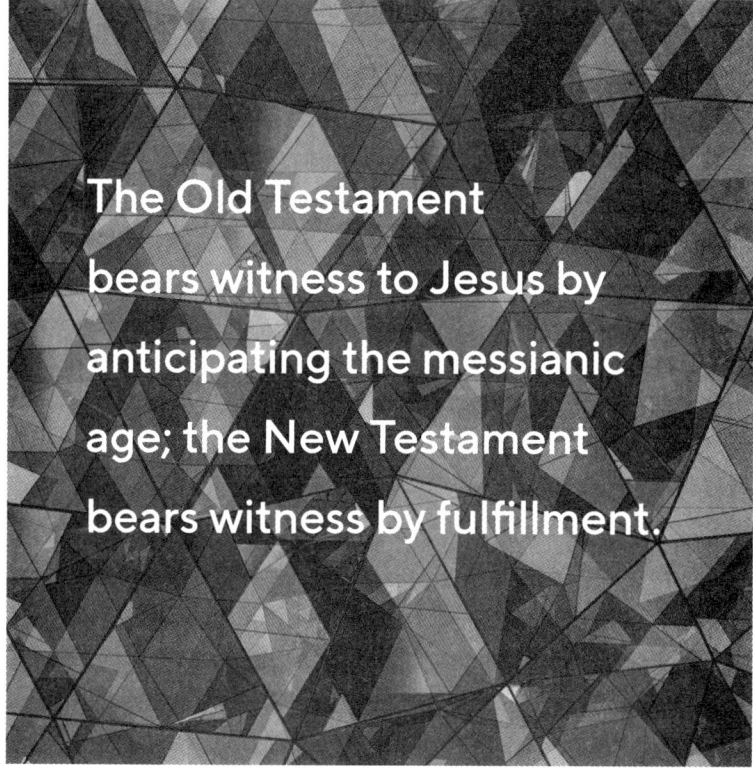

Revelation, the Trinity, and the Bible

Jesus Christ is revelation—the Word of God in the strict and primary sense; however, the Bible is the Word of God in a secondary and derived sense because, like the prophetic word and the apostles' preaching, it bears witness to Jesus. So, just as revelation has a Trinitarian structure, so the Bible's authority also has a Trinitarian structure.

The authority of the Bible rests upon its character as inspired witness to revelation—which means the Bible is the written record of the attempt by God's people (both Israel and the early Christian church) to serve the Word of God. In some cases, this service takes the form of law codes; in other cases, it appears as prophetic speech; in still other cases, it occurs as narrative or in other forms. But in every case, the people of God sought to bear witness to revelation by passing on traditions, narrating sacred events, and teaching with inspired wisdom. In the ultimate sense, the Bible is a record of the people of God's service to Jesus Christ—the incarnate Word. The Old Testament bears witness to Jesus by anticipating the messianic age; the New Testament bears witness by fulfillment. The Bible's authority is accordingly dependent on its relation to revelation—to Jesus Christ.

Just as revelation must be received and actualized in human life in order to be revelation, so the Bible must be actualized in our lives in order to be authoritative. As the Holy Spirit actualizes our communion with God in acts of rebirth and sanctification, so the Spirit makes the Bible become for us the living Word of God. Without the Spirit's illumination, the Bible remains a dead letter, an ancient book, just as, without the Spirit sanctifying us, Jesus Christ remains revelation only in an objective—not in a fully realized—sense. The Bible's authority rests on its relation to the Holy Spirit as well as on its relation to Jesus Christ.

Finally, the Bible's authority rests on its relation to God the Father. Ultimately, the Bible is about God the Father's quest to create communion with humanity. In the Old Testament, the Father does so by giving the Spirit and by speaking the prophetic word. This quest culminates in sending the Son into the world and by giving the Holy Spirit to the church. The Bible is, therefore, a narrative in three parts: creation, alienation, and communion. The substance of this narrative is the Father's project of achieving communion with humankind and with all creation. The Bible's authority is a function of its faithfully telling this story.

FOUR · The Trinity and Creation

The Old Testament

No Christian doctrine makes sense without the doctrine of the Trinity. Chapter 3 showed the Trinitarian structure of revelation. It is now time to address the doctrine that seems to have the least connection with the Trinity—the doctrine of creation.

The doctrine of creation has traditionally been drawn from the Old Testament; the doctrine of the Trinity has traditionally been drawn from the New Testament. One seems to have little to do with the other. Yet, when properly understood, the idea of creation is profoundly Trinitarian, for the God who creates and recreates is Father, Son, and Spirit.

We begin with a logical starting point—the opening chapters of Genesis. But this classical creation text already shows us an initial Trinitarian form, for in these chapters God speaks the Word and breathes forth the Spirit.

In chapter 1, God creates by speaking. God speaks, and something comes into being. This reminds us of what is said about God's word in Isaiah 55:10–11: "As the rain and the snow come down from heaven, and do not return to it without watering the earth and making it bud and flourish, so that it yields seed for the sower and bread for the eater, so is my word that goes out from my mouth: It will not return to me empty, but will accomplish what I desire and achieve the purpose for which I sent it."

God's speech is inherently creative; the word thus becomes the characteristic way in which God acts. So it is not surprising when we read in the first chapter of John that the divine Word was in the beginning with God and that all things came into being through the Word (John 1:1-3). From the perspective of John's Gospel, the creation story found in Genesis is already thoroughly christological and, hence, Trinitarian. (Christology simply refers to the theological study of Christ.)

The christological connotation of creation is reinforced by the association between God's word and God's wisdom. We see this connection in Proverbs 8, which speaks of personified wisdom being with God before the creation of the world and being present when God created (vv. 22-31). In Psalm 104, God is said to have made all things with wisdom (v. 24). We see here a confluence of ideas: God possesses wisdom; God creates using this wisdom; God creates by speaking; the divine word is an expression of God's wisdom. Once again, there is a christological association, for Jesus Christ is the wisdom of God (1 Corinthians 1:24, 30).

We can see, then, that the first chapter of Genesis, when read in the light of the New Testament, is an act of both God the Father and also the Son, the Word and Wisdom of God.

As we proceed to Genesis 2, we see in the second account of creation God breathing the breath of life into clay to form a living human being (v. 7). But what does breath (the Hebrew word is *neshamah*) have to do with the Trinity? If breath means physical breath, then the answer is nothing. However, passages such as Genesis 7:22 and Job 34:14 show us that the meaning of "breath" converges with the meaning of "spirit" (the Hebrew word is *ruah*). For example, Psalm 104:29–30 speaks of God taking away the *ruah* of creatures, causing them to die, and sending forth the divine *ruah*, causing things to be created. In Genesis 1:2, the *ruah* of God hovers over the primordial water, preparing it for God's creative acts. The Old Testament comfortably interchanges "breath" and "spirit," seeing both as (1) the principle by which creatures live and (2) a gift from God.

The Trinitarian connection lies in how the Old Testament sees God's spirit and/or breath as a source of life. Of course, this conception is not a complete presentation of the idea of the Holy Spirit. It is, at most, an intimation. However, as the biblical tradition develops into the New Testament, this notion of God's breath and/or spirit entering humans and creating life eventually assumes fuller form as the New Testament's affirmations about the Holy Spirit being the source of new life in Christ.

When we read the Old Testament, we do not expect to find fully developed Christian beliefs. Nonetheless, the seeds of those beliefs can always be found. In this way, the Old Testament's teaching about creation bears witness to God in a way that anticipates the New Testament's affirmations about God's creative power, manifested in the divine Word and Spirit.

The New Testament

It may seem that the New Testament says little about creation, because it lacks a stately passage such as Genesis 1-2. It is true that the emphasis in the New Testament rests on the new thing that God has done in Jesus Christ and that there is no sustained teaching about creation. However, there are two important points to keep in mind: First, what the New Testament says about creation may be brief, but it is important. Second, we will miss the New Testament's full teaching about creation unless we keep in mind the way creation and new creation converge.

First, let us look at the New Testament's express statements about creation, asking how they exhibit a Trinitarian structure.

God the Father and Creation

The New Testament consistently portrays God the Father as the origin of all things. Consider these passages:

- "From him and through him and for him are all things" (Rom. 11:36a).
- ". . . there is but one God, the Father, from whom all things came . . ." (1 Cor. 8:6a).
- "Everything comes from God" (1 Cor. 11:12b).
- ". . . God, for whom and through whom everything exists . . ." (Heb. 2:10b).

Creation is not the work of God the Father alone; the Father creates through the Son and by the Holy Spirit. However, the distinctive role of God the Father is the ultimate source of all things. The Father's role as the ultimate source parallels the Father's eschatological (end-of-days) role as the ultimate goal, or *telos* in the Greek, of creation. As Paul stated, "Then the end will come, when he [Jesus Christ] hands over the kingdom to God the Father after he has destroyed all dominion, authority and power. For he must reign until he has put all his enemies under his feet. . . . When he has done this, then the Son himself will be made subject to him who put everything under him, so that God may be all in all" (1 Cor. 15:24–25, 28).

While this remarkable passage transcends our complete understanding, clearly all creation will, as redeemed, eventually render to God its perfect worship (Rom. 8:19–

21). God will complete God's purposes. In the fulfilled new creation—the consummated kingdom—God will, as originally intended, dwell with God's people, and they with God (Rev. 21:2-4).[1] Ephesians 1 says that in Christ, the Father of our Lord Jesus Christ is unifying all things, "to the praise of his glorious grace," things "in heaven and on earth" (see vv. 3-10). Colossians 1 concurs: in Christ, the Father is now reconciling all things to himself, "whether things on earth or things in heaven, by making peace through his blood, shed on the cross" (v. 20). All things come from the Father, and eventually all things will be— *through* Christ and *by* the Holy Spirit—restored to the Father. John Wesley referred to this as breathing back to God the life we have received. The creative and redemptive circle will be complete (Rev. 1:5b-7; 21:1-8).

The lesson to draw from this is that the doctrine of creation must be studied in connection with eschatology (last things) and eschatology in connection with creation. The end cannot be understood apart from the beginning, nor the beginning apart from the end, for the two coincide in the rule of God the Father in his consummation of the kingdom inaugurated by Jesus. When "return" is subsequently discussed in this book, it should be understood in these eschatological, "new creation" terms.[2]

God the Son and Creation

Jesus Christ is the agent of creation. We have already noted the affirmation of John 1:3 that everything came into

---

1. For a thorough explanation of Genesis chapters 2-3 as portraying God ordering the world as a temple—sacred space—for God's dwelling, and for humankind's intended priestly role, see John H. Walton, *The Lost World of Adam and Eve: Genesis 2-3 and the Human Origins Debate* (Downers Grove, IL: InterVarsity Press, 2015).

2. See N. T. Wright, *Surprised by Hope: Rethinking Heaven, the Resurrection, and the Mission of the Church* (New York: HarperOne, 2008), especially pp. 101-108.

being through the Word and that without the Word nothing at all came into being. John's Gospel here expressly refers back to the creative word of Genesis 1. Jesus Christ is the enfleshment of God's eternal, creative Word. Additionally, we have Hebrews 1:2, which tells us that God the Father created *through* the Son, and Colossians 1:16, according to which everything in heaven and on earth was created in (or with) Jesus Christ. These texts ground the doctrine of creation firmly in Christology.

Yet it is not as though Jesus Christ is the Creator alone. On the contrary, Trinitarian theology requires us to see that every divine act begins with God the Father, takes places in and through the Son, and comes to completion in the Holy Spirit. With respect to creation, we can say that God the Father is the ultimate source of all things; Jesus Christ is the agent or means—the creative Word—by which God the Father creates; and the Holy Spirit brings creation to completion by actualizing the new creation in the human heart. In the words of Paul, "Yet for us there is but one God, the Father, from whom all things came and for whom we live; and there is but one Lord, Jesus Christ, through whom all things came and through whom we live" (1 Cor. 8:6). This verse captures the Father's role as source ("*from* whom") and *telos* ("*for* whom"); it also captures Jesus's role as agent or means ("*through* whom"). Our understanding of Christ's role as agent is amplified by the New Testament's confession that Jesus Christ is the wisdom of God. His status as wisdom, with its background in such texts as Psalm 104:24 (God has made everything with wisdom) and Proverbs 3:19 (God established the earth by wisdom and the heavens by understanding) give us a more concrete picture of the Son's role in creation.

Jesus Christ, then, is both the Word *and* the Wisdom of God. God creates by speaking: Jesus Christ is the speech of God. God creates with wisdom; Jesus Christ is God's wisdom. Creation, then, is not simply the act of God the Father; creation cannot be rightly understood apart from Christology, just as it cannot be grasped without considering eschatology.

God the Spirit and Creation

The New Testament refers directly to the creative activity of God the Father and of Jesus Christ; however, it does not explicitly reference the role of the Holy Spirit in creation. In particular, there is no mention of the breath or spirit of life as in Genesis 2. Does that mean creation involves only the Father and the Son?

To see the Spirit's role in creation, we must proceed indirectly. We note that the Spirit is instrumental in the virginal conception (Matt. 1:18; Luke 1:35) and that the Spirit is the agent of resurrection (Rom. 8:11). These passages hint at the creative power of the Spirit; they suggest that, as in Genesis 2, the Holy Spirit is the source of life, just as in Genesis 2 the breath and/or spirit of God turns lifeless dirt into something living. Additionally, in the stories about Jesus's baptism (e.g., Mark 1:10), the Spirit seems to hover above the water in a way that reminds us of the divine wind or spirit hovering over the primordial water in Genesis 1:2, preparing the water for the exercise of God's creative power.

More importantly, we remember that creation and new creation coincide. We see this expressly stated in Isaiah 40–55. Here God is frequently portrayed as the Creator (see, for example, Isa. 40:12–29; 42:5–9; 44:24; 45:7–12, 18; 48:13; and 51:13–16). God's status as Creator is the basis for Israel's redemption:

> For your Maker is your husband—the Lord Almighty is his name—the Holy One of Israel is your Redeemer; he is called the God of all the earth.
> (Isa. 54:5)

This is what the LORD says—your Redeemer, who formed you in the womb: I am the LORD, the Maker of all things, who stretches out the heavens, who spreads out the earth by myself . . . who says of Jerusalem, 'It shall be inhabited,' of the towns of Judah, 'They shall be rebuilt,' and of their ruins, 'I will restore them.' (Isa. 44:24, 26b)

These passages tell us that God is Israel's redeemer precisely because God is the Creator. New creation is grounded in original creation. God, who created in the beginning, will not allow creation to go unredeemed; Israel has no other redeemer than its Creator.

The confluence of creation and new creation is evident also in the New Testament, most obviously in the book of Revelation, with its vision of new heavens and a new earth (21:1) and its declaration that God is making all things new (21:5). Salvation, in other words, is depicted as the renewal of creation. The new creation is, moreover, a return to God's original purpose for creation. That is why Revelation mentions the tree of life as located in the new heaven and new earth (Rev. 22:2; cf. Gen. 2:15–17). New creation is not the rejection of original creation but its redemption, its transformation. Therefore, when we search the New Testament asking about the Spirit's role in creation, we must think not of old creation but of new creation and renewal. Thinking in this way leads us to consider passages such as these:

- "No one can enter the kingdom of God unless they are born of water and the Spirit" (John 3:5b).
- "He [God] saved us through the washing of rebirth and renewal by the Holy Spirit" (Titus 3:5b).

As previously noted, 1 Peter 1:2 and 2 Thessalonians 2:13 describe the Spirit as the agent of sanctification, which is the continuation and completion of rebirth. All these passages tell us that the Holy Spirit actualizes the new creation within us; the Spirit creates us anew in Jesus Christ.

Conclusion

Like every Christian doctrine, creation in its fully Christian sense is understandable only if we grasp its Trinitarian structure. Creation is an act of the triune God. God the Father is the origin and *telos* (goal) of all things. God the Son is the creative Word and Wisdom by which the Father creates. God the Holy Spirit is the agent of life in all its forms, especially of the new creation.

FIVE

The Trinity and Salvation

What is salvation? This concept, which seems so straightforward and simple, is in fact subject to notable distortion, especially in American evangelicalism. The roots of this distortion are many and complex, but the result is clear: in place of the Bible's well-rounded understanding, salvation is often portrayed in emaciated form, reduced to a dramatic conversion experience or receiving forgiveness of sins. Conversion and forgiveness are indeed important facets of salvation, but they are far from its totality. To appreciate the full measure of salvation, it is instructive to hear John Wesley:

> Salvation begins with what is usually termed (and very properly) preventing grace; including the first wish to please God, the first dawn of light concerning his will, and the first slight transient conviction of having sinned against him. All these imply some tendency toward life; some degree of salvation; the beginning of a deliverance from a blind, unfeeling heart, quite insensible of God and the things of God. Salvation is carried on by convincing grace, usually in Scripture termed repentance; which brings a larger measure of self-knowledge, and a further deliverance from the

heart of stone. Afterwards we experience the proper Christian salvation; whereby, "through grace," we "are saved by faith;" consisting of those two grand branches, justification and sanctification. By justification we are saved from the guilt of sin, and restored to the favour of God; by sanctification we are saved from the power and root of sin, and restored to the image of God. All experience, as well as Scripture, shows this salvation to be both instantaneous and gradual. It begins the moment we are justified, in the holy, humble, gentle, patient love of God and man. It gradually increases from that moment, as "a grain of mustard-seed, which, at first, is the least of all seeds," but afterwards puts forth large branches, and becomes a great tree; till, in another instant, the heart is cleansed, from all sin, and filled with pure love to God and man. But even that love increases more and more, till we "grow up in all things into him that is our Head;" till we attain "the measure of the stature of the fullness of Christ."[1]

For Wesley, salvation is more than conversion or justification; it embraces the full range of God's actions toward us: awakening, repentance, conversion, justification, regeneration, adoption, sanctification, and finally glorification. Because salvation is so extensive, it requires the triune God. If salvation were only an act of forgiveness or the experience of conversion, a unitary God would suffice. But an authentically Christian conception of salvation makes sense only if God is triune. Salvation is not accomplished simply by God the Father or the Son alone or the Holy Spirit. Sal-

---

1. John Wesley, Sermon 85: "On Working Out Our Own Salvation," II, 1, http://wesley.nnu.edu/john-wesley/the-sermons-of-john-wesley-1872-edition/sermon-85-on-working-out-our-own-salvation/.

vation is an act of the three Persons of God acting in their inseparable unity.

To keep matters simple, in this chapter we will focus on salvation as it is presented in the New Testament; in this way we avoid the difficult question of the role of the Son and the Holy Spirit in the Old Testament—an important subject best reserved for more advanced treatments of the Trinity.

God the Father

The activity of God the Father in salvation is principally a matter of sending the Son into the world and raising Jesus from the dead and exalting him as Lord. This act is in accordance with the Father's role as the source from which all things come and to which all things return. The sending of the Son and Jesus's exaltation reproduce the movement whereby the created world comes forth from God and then eschatologically returns to God. The history of the Son—coming forth from the Father, returning to the Father—thus recapitulates the history of creation. The sending of the Son and his resurrection and exaltation constitute a new act of creation by God the Father, an act by which original creation is restored to God.

Jesus Christ

Jesus Christ is the focus of the New Testament's teaching about salvation. Every aspect of his life as presented in the New Testament bears on salvation. Here is a brief listing of these aspects and their significance for salvation:

- Incarnation
    - The Son gave up his riches so that we might gain riches (2 Cor. 8:9), and assumed human likeness, leaving us an example of humility (Phil. 2:3–8). Moreover, the Son shared in our nature,

even to the point of death, in order to defeat death (Heb. 2:14); he suffered and was tested in order to help us who suffer and are tested (Heb. 2:17–18; 4:15).

- Baptism
  - By submitting to baptism, Jesus gave us an example of righteousness and obedience (Matt. 3:13–15).
- Teaching
  - Jesus proclaimed the kingdom of God and the way of repentance and faith (Mark 1:15). Additionally, Jesus revealed God the Father (John 1:18).
- Founding the Christian Community
  - Jesus established the church as a community of love and of the Spirit (John 13:34; 14:15–17).
- Miracles
  - Jesus's miracles were works by which disciples were delivered from their bondage to the evil powers of the present age (Luke 13:10–16).
- The Son's Obedience
  - By submitting to death on a cross, Jesus rendered to God the Father an act of obedience resulting in justification and righteousness for all (Rom. 5:18–19).
- Suffering and Death
  - The New Testament uses a variety of metaphors to understand Jesus's death and its significance: redemption, blood atonement, ransom, the Suffering Servant mentioned in Isaiah, the Passover Lamb, and others. As a result of Christ's death, we have peace with God (Rom. 5:1), we are reconciled to God (Rom. 5:10), we are justified (Rom. 5:18), we have been delivered from the

present evil age (Gal. 1:3-4), we have been freed from slavery (Heb. 2:14), our consciences have been purified (Heb. 9:14), we have been sanctified (Heb. 10:14), we have been healed (1 Peter 2:24), and we have been cleansed from sin (1 John 1:7).

- Resurrection
  - Through Christ's resurrection we are born again (1 Peter 1:3); through the resurrection, baptism saves us (1 Peter 3:21). Moreover, we have eternal life because we participate in Jesus's resurrection (Rom. 6:4-5).
- State of Exaltation
  - As the exalted Lord, Jesus acts as high priest and mediator between God the Father and humankind (1 Tim. 2:5; Heb. 7:24-26).
- Pouring out the Holy Spirit
  - Jesus, with the Father, sends the Holy Spirit upon the church, beginning to actualize salvation in the lives of believers (John 20:22; Acts 2:33).
- Return of Christ
  - Christ's second coming will bring salvation to its fulfillment (Titus 2:13; Heb. 9:28; 1 Peter 1:5).

Jesus Christ has particular importance with respect to sanctification. The key to understanding sanctification is to see its connection with the image of God. In the postbiblical tradition of Christian thought, the idea of humankind's creation in the image of God proved to be a highly useful way of thinking about human nature and also about the corrupting effects of sin. Corruption is thus understood as damage done to our status as the image of God—which is why the New Testament's identification of Jesus Christ as the image of God is so important. Genesis 1 affirms that humankind bears the image of God; however, the New Testament insists that Jesus is the *true* image of God. In other words, although humans at least originally showed forth God's nature, under the condition of sin, it is only Jesus—the sinless one—who authentically and powerfully images God.

Jesus's status as the image of God forms the basis for the doctrine of sanctification, as when Paul wrote about our being "predestined to be conformed to the image" of the Son (Rom. 8:29) and our "being transformed into his image" (2 Cor. 3:18). Elsewhere, Colossians speaks of "the new self" that is "being renewed" in accordance with the "image of its Creator" (Col. 3:10), and Ephesians states the new self has been created according to the likeness of God (Eph. 4:24). Finally, sanctification as the restoration of our status as the image of God has an eschatological dimension, as Paul noted when he contrasted our bearing the image of Adam with the fact that, in the future, we will fully bear the image of Jesus (1 Cor. 15:47–49), just as, according to 2 Corinthians 3:18, we are even now being transformed.

According to the framework of the biblical narrative, then, humankind begins its history as bearers of the image of God. As a result of sin, our status as image bearers is lost, or at least distorted; we live under the corruption of human nature. God then sends the Son into the world as the prototype of the image of God—"the last Adam," to use Paul's phrase (1 Cor. 15:45). Salvation consists in our becoming conformed to Jesus Christ, who is the perfect image of God. In this way, our own status as image bearers comes to be redefined and restored.

The Holy Spirit

As we have seen, the Holy Spirit is the Creator Spirit, to use the words of an ancient hymn (*"Veni, Creator Spiritus"*). But in the Bible, creation looks forward to the new creation (Isa. 65:17–25; 66:22–23; Rom. 8:18–21; Rev. 21:1–8). The new creation is the restoration of God's original creation. The Holy Spirit is, accordingly, the Spirit of the new creation, active in every step of the new life in Christ. Let's survey some of the main themes related to the Spirit's role in the new creation.

The Holy Spirit and the New Birth

We learn much about the Spirit's redemptive work by reflecting on verses such as 2 Corinthians 3:6: "He has made us competent as ministers of a new covenant—not of the letter but of the Spirit; for the letter kills, but the Spirit gives life;" and Romans 8:11: "And if the Spirit of him who raised Jesus from the dead is living in you, he who raised Christ from the dead will also give life to your mortal bodies because of his Spirit who lives in you."

As we saw in chapter 4, it is characteristic of the Holy Spirit to be the agent of life, originally in creation, but especially in new creation. The Spirit accomplishes the new birth (or, regeneration): God "saved us through the washing of rebirth and renewal by the Holy Spirit" (Titus 3:5b). This passage from Titus tells us that in baptism we are reborn and renewed and that the Spirit is the renewer. John 3:5 makes a similar point: we cannot enter God's kingdom unless we are born of water and the Spirit. In baptism, we are washed, reborn, and renewed in spiritual life. All of this is the Spirit's work, bringing to perfection the redemption accomplished by Jesus Christ.

The Holy Spirit as the Spirit of Adoption

The Spirit is the Spirit not only of renewal but also of adoption. As members of the body of Christ, we become God's children. With this new status comes a new Spirit—the Spirit of adoption, by which we leave behind fear and attain familiarity with God (Rom. 8:14–16; Gal. 4:6).

Changing metaphors, Ephesians speaks of the Spirit as a seal (Eph. 1:13–14; 4:30). In ancient times, letters and other documents were written on long sheets and then rolled up. Wax was applied to the edge and a stamp pushed into the wax, forming a seal. The purpose of the seal was to indicate ownership or authenticity. With this metaphor, Ephesians is saying that God has sealed Christian disciples with the Holy Spirit, showing that we belong to God.

The Holy Spirit and Assurance

Feeling the Spirit of adoption within us, we are assured of our standing with God. In the words of 1 John, we know that God lives in us because God has given us the Spirit (1 John 3:24; 4:13). Or as Paul put it, our hope in God will not be disappointed because the Spirit has poured God's love into our hearts (Rom. 5:5). For Paul, the experience of Spirit-inspired love is proof that our hope is well placed.

The connection between the Spirit and our sense of assurance is developed in New Testament texts that refer to the Spirit as a pledge or down payment (2 Cor. 1:21–22; 2 Cor. 5:5; and Eph. 1:14). The idea here is that, as we wait for the return of Jesus, God has given us the Spirit as a down payment that guarantees the eventual fulfillment of the kingdom of God. Paul made the same point by referring to the Spirit as the "firstfruits." Firstfruits of what? Of the end—the fulfillment of God's kingdom and the messianic age (Rom. 8:23). The Holy Spirit is the way we experience the kingdom of God now, in advance of the complete appearance of the kingdom when Jesus returns.

The Spirit's status as a pledge of the future kingdom is another way of saying that the Holy Spirit is an eschatological reality—the fact that we have received the Holy Spirit means that the end times have already begun. In other words, the giving of the Spirit signifies that the messianic age and the kingdom of God have already become powerfully effective in human history. That is why Acts saw the giving of the Spirit two thousand years ago as a fulfillment of Joel's prophecy about the end-time pouring-out of God's Spirit (Acts 2:16–21).

Because life in the Spirit is an eschatological reality, those in the Spirit receive, in a tentative and preliminary way, the eschatological blessings of the kingdom of God: Spirit-inspired comfort (Acts 9:31), life and peace (Rom. 8:6), hope (Rom. 15:13), and joy (1 Thess. 1:6).

The Holy Spirit and Sanctification

The Holy Spirit is the Spirit of regeneration, adoption, and assurance. But the Spirit is also the agent of sanctification:

- The Spirit performs the circumcision of the heart that enables us to love and obey God (Rom. 2:29; see also Deut. 30:6; Jer. 4:4).
- We have been washed, justified, and sanctified with the Spirit (1 Cor. 6:11).
- God has chosen us for salvation by means of the Spirit's sanctification (2 Thess. 2:13).
- We have been chosen according to God the Father's foreknowledge, with the Spirit's sanctification, for obedience to Jesus Christ (1 Peter 1:1–2).

There are other important dimensions of sanctification. One is that, now being holy, we have access, in the Spirit, to God (Eph. 1:18; cf. Heb. 10:19–22). In the condition of sin, we are alienated from God. But as we live in the Spirit and experience the Spirit's sanctifying power, we are able to approach the holy God in the power of the Spirit.

The sanctifying transition from death to life can also be expressed as the movement from flesh to Spirit. In the Bible, "flesh" signifies creaturely existence insofar as it exists on its own, out of relationship with God. The flesh is, therefore, not simply the body. Instead, to say we are flesh is to say we are weak creatures subject to death, spiritual travail, and failings of all sorts. But to be flesh is not simply equivalent to the condition of sin. Instead, it characterizes human existence conducted apart from the Spirit of God—an existence distinctly susceptible to the power of sin. It describes human existence in the old age that is being eclipsed by the new, messianic age of the Spirit.

Another important consequence of the sanctifying work of the Spirit, and connected to the theme of regeneration, is that the Spirit gives life (see John 6:63; 2 Cor. 3:6). Existence in the flesh is a state of death: the body is subject to corruption; the human spirit dwells in a deathlike state of spiritual darkness. By contrast, to be in the Spirit is to receive new life—we are born anew. Having been brought from death to life, we now live to God (Rom. 6:11–13). This infusion of life will eventually result in the resurrection of the body, which God accomplishes through the Spirit (Rom. 8:11; 1 Cor. 15:42–57).

So, the New Testament consistently contrasts life in the flesh with life in the Spirit: some are born of the flesh; others are born of the Spirit (John 3:6); the flesh is hostile to God, and those in the flesh cannot please God (Rom. 8:7–8); the flesh and the Spirit stand opposed, with opposite desires (Gal. 5:17). Walking in step with the Spirit is the alternative to life in the flesh. By living in the power of the Spirit, we avoid fulfilling the desires of the flesh (Gal. 5:16) and instead show forth the Spirit's fruit (Gal. 5:22–23). Abounding in the Spirit's fruit, we fulfill God's righteous decrees (Rom. 8:4)—something that is impossible for those who live according to the flesh.

Further Considerations

We have so far briefly reviewed some of the New Testament's affirmations about salvation. These texts reveal a clear

Trinitarian pattern to salvation: salvation comes to us from God, through the mediation of Jesus Christ, and is actualized in us by the power of the Holy Spirit. However, it is possible and in fact salutary to move beyond accumulating scriptural passages to grasp the Trinitarian logic of salvation—to see how salvation is grounded in God's Trinitarian life.

Let's begin with a consideration of sin. Because the Bible contains many imperatives (e.g., the Ten Commandments and other legal material), it is natural to imagine that sin primarily consists of violating God's commands. Such a view is not wholly wrong, but it misses the most important aspect of sin—namely, that sin is a *condition* before it is an *act*. The act does not appear from nowhere; it is grounded in the condition of the soul. If sin were simply a matter of action, then salvation would consist in nothing more than correcting one's conduct and receiving divine forgiveness and mercy. But if sin is a condition that gives rise to action, then it requires more than forgiveness. It requires healing and restoration. It requires sanctification.

In the biblical and Christian tradition, the condition of sin has been understood in two fundamental ways: (1) corruption, and (2) alienation. Paul described the condition of corruption in Romans 7, where he depicted human existence as a state of slavery to sin in which there is no good within us. The result is that we cannot do what is good (Rom. 7:14–20). Alienation is portrayed in passages that describe humankind apart from Christ as children of wrath (Eph. 2:3) and that say humankind dwells in a state of estrangement (Col. 1:21). This alienation operates at two levels: (1) We are without God, and (2) we are also alienated from one another—Gentiles from Jews, for instance (Eph. 2:12).

When the condition of sin is portrayed as corruption, salvation takes the form of healing or sanctification. When we think of sin as alienation, then salvation appears as reconciliation or the restoration of communion. Both of these—sanctification and reconciliation—bear a Trinitarian stamp and structure.

The Restoration of Communion

If we conceive of sin as alienation, then salvation appears as reconciliation. However, it is important to grasp what the Bible means by reconciliation. After a war, for instance, it is possible for nations to be reconciled in the sense that they cease hostilities and reestablish diplomatic relations. Or political opponents may be publicly reconciled after a bitter election. But when we are dealing with God's reconciliation with the world, the matter is different. In national or political reconciliations, the two parties often remain, even in reconciliation, outside each other—enclosed and separate. Their peace is merely external; their harmony is only public. But God's reconciliation involves communion and fellowship. The Greek word is *koinonia*, which is related to the word *koinos*. *Koinos* means "common"—that is, that which is shared by many.

God's reconciliation with the world involves establishing communion with the world. In reconciliation, we not only have peace with God, but we also share in God. We become, in a finite way, *like* God—imitators of God (Eph. 5:1). In the words of 2 Peter, we become sharers in (*koinonia*) the divine nature (2 Peter 1:4). The importance of communion, of sharing in God, is signaled in many ways in the New Testament. Consider these passages:

- We have been baptized into Christ's death (Rom. 6:3).
- We have been crucified with Christ (Rom. 6:6).
- We have become married to Christ (Rom. 7:4).

- Our bodies are members of Christ's body (1 Cor. 6:19).
- The community of Christian believers is collectively the body of Christ (1 Cor. 12:12, 27).
- We daily carry in our bodies both Christ's death and his resurrected life (2 Cor. 4:10).
- It is no longer we who live but Christ who lives in us (Gal. 2:20).
- Christ is being formed within us (Gal. 4:19).
- We share in the sufferings of Christ (Phil. 3:10).
- We have been buried with Christ (Col. 2:12).
- We have been resurrected with Christ (Col. 3:1).

These and similar texts add up to a weighty affirmation that God's communion with us is a matter of our sharing in the death and resurrected life of Christ—hence Paul's frequent use of the phrase "in Christ." From the perspective of the New Testament, our former, earthly life according to the flesh has come to an end, and we now share in the life of Jesus.

The idea of communion receives its fullest exposition in the Gospel of John, which carefully establishes the absolute unity of Father and Son (10:30, 38; 14:10) and then presents salvation as a matter of believers dwelling in the Son (14:20; 15:4). Finally, salvation is depicted as disciples being drawn into the fellowship of the Father and the Son:

> Holy Father, protect them by the power of your name, the name you gave me, so that they may be one as we are one. . . . My prayer is not for them alone. I pray also for those who will believe in me through their message, that all of them may be one, Father, just as you are in me and I am in you. May they also be in us so that the world may believe that you have sent me. I have given them the glory that you gave me, that they may be one, as we are one—I in them and you in me—so that they may be brought to complete unity. Then

the world will know that you have sent me and have
loved them even as you have loved me.
(John 17:11b, 20-23)

This important passage tells us that God's ultimate goal for God's people is that they dwell in the same unity and communion that exist eternally between the Father and the Son. The earthly community of disciples must exhibit the love and unity that characterize the eternal relation between Father and Son. Such love and unity would be one of the principal forms of witness to the world—for when the world sees love and unity in the church, it will actually be seeing the love and unity of the Father and the Son.

But how do we enter into the fellowship of the Father and the Son? How do we come to abide in Christ? To answer those questions, we must return to a previous consideration. We have noted that God the Father is both the origin and the *telos* (goal) of all things. All things come from God the Father, and all things return to the Father through the mediation of Jesus Christ. Creation is thus a grand cycle, a movement of coming forth and returning. The coming forth—the creation—is simply an act of God; God's will alone explains the coming forth of all things. But how is it possible for all things to return to God? This particularity is especially problematic in the case of humans, who existentially dwell in a state of corruption and alienation. Something more than a divine decree is required in order for humankind to return to God. It is not enough for God to *will* our return; we must participate. But in our fallen state of corruption and alienation, we cannot execute this return. We lack the capacity to turn back to God on our own.

Consequently, God must bring about our return. This is the work of the Holy Spirit, who reverses the corruption of our nature in sanctification and who draws us into the eternal communion of the Father and the Son. That is why Paul linked the Holy Spirit to communion (2 Cor. 13:14 and Phil. 2:1).

Sanctification and Communion

Earlier in this chapter we looked at sanctification in terms of the image of God. However, now that we have explored the idea of communion, let's look again at sanctification, this time in terms of communion.

Let us consider a text we have seen before, 2 Peter 1:4, which declares that we are partakers of the divine nature. This passage tells us that God is more than just a being we should imitate. On the contrary, God's being is such that we can *share* in that being. God's own life is one of communion. Some theologians have used the term *perichoresis* to describe God's life of communion; the term suggests the image of dancers moving about one another. Salvation consists in sharing in that communion. That is why Johannine texts affirm that we abide in God (John 15:4) and that those who abide in love abide in God (1 John 4:16). Such abiding in God is possible only because God *is* self-giving love (1 John 4:8). Because love is communion, God's being, which is love, is communion, and is therefore a reality in which we can share.

This is the basis for claiming that sanctification is love. It is so because it is the perfection of our participation in God, whose life is a life of love and communion. The life of holiness is a life in which the Trinity lives in us and leads us into acts of love and communion. We attain a holy character to the extent that we actualize our participation in God's Trinitarian life of love and communion. This is why the New Testament regards love as the greatest of all the commandments (Mark 12:28–31), as the summary of all the commandments (Rom 13:8–10), and as the measure of our perfection (Matt. 5:48). Because God is love, holy character is a matter of sharing in and being formed by God's character. When we love our neighbor or enemy, we share in God's Trinitarian love toward the other and in God's Trinitarian movement into the world. When we love, we create communion and realize God's healing presence in the world.

Of course, it is important to remember that love consists in concrete acts of goodness. When Jesus gave an example of loving the neighbor in the parable of the Good Samaritan, he spoke of deeds of kindness. Even more strongly, 1 John speaks of laying down our lives for each other, sharing material goods with each other, and loving with deeds instead of speech (3:16–18).

At the same time, it is important to remember that love is not *only* acts of goodness. It is, more fundamentally, the sharing of life, just as the Father dwells in the Son and the Son in the Father. When we love our neighbors by performing acts of goodness, we are creating a relationship of communion. In this relationship we no longer insist on doing what is good for us individually. Instead, we think of others as more important than ourselves and seek the good of our neighbors instead of our own good (Phil. 2:3–4). In this way we imitate Jesus, who emptied himself for our good (Phil. 2:5–8) and we abide in the God who is love (1 John 4:16).

Sanctification, accordingly, is more than upright behavior or even godly character. It is, above all, sharing in God's life of love and communion, and extending that love and communion to others.

The Triune God and Salvation

Like revelation and creation, salvation also has a Trinitarian structure. In particular, salvation is our participation in the fellowship between the Father and the Son in the power of the Spirit; sanctification is becoming conformed to Jesus Christ, who is the image of God, through the ministry of the Holy Spirit.

Because salvation is a matter of sanctification and reconciliation, it requires that God be more than a unitary being. If salvation is a matter of entering into the life of God, which is a life of communion, God must be a Trinity—the Father and Son, who dwell in an eternal life of love, unity, and communion, and the Holy Spirit, who leads us into participation in the eternal love, unity, and communion.

Considering salvation in light of its Trinitarian structure tells us much about salvation, but it also tells us much about the triune God, especially when we meditate on the narrative of creation's coming forth from God and returning to God. It tells us not only that creation comes forth from God but also that God goes forth into the world. God doesn't remain in heaven, directing human salvation like the director of a play. On the contrary, this narrative says that God enters into the world and unites with the world in the incarnation of the Word. Moreover, this union is not superficial. God does not merely visit the world or pass through. Instead, God so thoroughly unites with the world that God becomes human and experiences death. By the sending forth of the Son into the world, God becomes that which is not God: suffering, dying, and identifying with sinful humankind. Yet God does so without ceasing to be God. God does not simply become human; God becomes human *and* remains God. In the death of Jesus Christ God confronts death and takes it into the divine life. In Jesus Christ God dies, but really it is death that dies. Death is not the death of God; God is the end of death and remains the eternal source of life and new life. Further, God sends forth the Holy Spirit so that God's union and communion with humankind can become universal, actual, in every individual.

The narrative of coming forth and returning tells us that God's life is not only a life of communion but also of movement. God comes into the world by sending the Son and then the Holy Spirit. And, God causes the return of creation to its unity with God through the power of the Holy Spirit. The movement that characterizes God's relation to the world is, in fact, intrinsic to God's being. The eternal life of the triune God is simultaneously communion and movement.

six The Trinity and the Church

Like revelation, creation, and salvation, the church has a Trinitarian structure—because the church is more than a voluntary association of people. Humans gather together in many sorts of chosen communities—clubs, business associations, political parties, and so on. All of these have some purpose, and most produce some good; however, from a theological perspective we put the Christian church in a different category. It does indeed have a voluntary aspect, but it is more than that because of its Trinitarian character.

God the Father and the Church

As previously noted, all things come from and return to God the Father. How does the church fit into this movement? First, the church has its origin in God. Like ancient Israel, the church is the holy people of God, chosen by God for God's purposes (1 Peter 2:9) and God's household (Eph. 2:19; 1 Tim. 3:15; 1 Peter 4:17). The existence of the church is grounded in the being of God. Second, the church participates in the return of all things to God. It does so by leading all things in their return to God through acts of praise—worship being the concrete form. The church is thus a royal priesthood (1 Peter 2:9), offering a sacrifice of praise to God the Father (Heb. 13:15).

In this connection, it is important to observe that in the New Testament, praise and worship are consistently directed *to* God the Father *through* Jesus Christ:

- "To the only wise God be glory forever through Jesus Christ! Amen" (Rom. 16:27).
- "Always giving thanks to God the Father for everything, in the name of our Lord Jesus Christ" (Eph. 5:20).
- "And whatever you do, whether in word or deed, do it all in the name of the Lord Jesus, giving thanks to God the Father through him" (Col. 3:17).
- "To the only God our Savior be glory, majesty, power and authority, through Jesus Christ our Lord, before all ages, now and forevermore! Amen" (Jude 1:25).

These passages show us that worship—the characteristic act of the church—is directed to God the Father in and through Jesus Christ. It thus has a distinctly Trinitarian structure.

Jesus Christ and the Church

The New Testament asserts the christological basis of the church. The church is, for instance, the household of God the Father with Jesus Christ being the cornerstone (Eph. 2:19–22). This building metaphor tells us that the church rests on Christ as its chief authority. Other metaphors, however, point us toward a more intimate and internal relationship between Christ and the church.

The church is the *body* of Christ. The resurrected Christ is a corporate reality, whose body on earth is the church and whose head is in heaven (Eph. 1:22–23). According to this organic metaphor, the entire body—the church—grows and builds itself from its head, Christ (Eph. 4:15–16). The growth and well-being of the church depend on its living connection with its head, Jesus Christ. The same point is made with the metaphor of the vine and branches. Just as the branch abides in the vine, so the church abides in Christ. Just as the branches cannot bear fruit without a connection to the vine, so the church cannot bear its fruit without being connected to Jesus (John 15:1–8).

The church is also the bride of Christ (1 Cor. 11:1–3; Eph. 5:21–32). This metaphor likewise asserts the greatest degree of union and intimacy between Christ and the church. In the words of Genesis 2, in marriage, Christ and the church have become one flesh, not to be divided.

These metaphors, especially the church as the body of Christ and the spouse of Christ, lead us to see the church as a reality that shares in God's movement from the Father in Jesus Christ.

The Holy Spirit and the Church

The church is a christological reality. It is organically united to Christ as a body is to its head. But because of the intimacy of the union between Christ and the church—because the church shares one common Spirit with Jesus Christ—the Spirit of Christ is also the Spirit of the church. The church is, accordingly, a reality grounded in the Holy Spirit—a *pneumatological* reality (we get the word "pneumatological" from the Greek word for Spirit, *pneuma*). So, when Ephesians tells us to maintain the unity of the Spirit, it means we should maintain the unity of the church, for the Holy Spirit is the church's unity, maintaining its unity with Christ, its head—there is one body and one Spirit (Eph. 4:4, 13). Consequently, the church is the temple of the Spirit—the Spirit's dwelling place (1 Cor. 3:16). The Spirit is the divine power at work in the church. Through the Spirit we have been baptized into one body, the church

(1 Cor. 12:13), and in the Spirit we all have access to God the Father (Eph. 2:18).

The church has its origin in God the Father's will to have a holy people, a royal priesthood who will lead the chorus of creation in worship back to God. The church is, additionally, a christological reality—the earthly manifestation of Christ's resurrected being, "the fullness of him who fills everything in every way" (Eph. 1:23). Finally, because the church is Christ's body, it shares in the Holy Spirit of Christ. Its existence as a unity, endowed with spiritual gifts, is due to its status as the house or temple of the Spirit.

God's Trinitarian Being and the Church

The passages we have reviewed give plenty of evidence that the church has a Trinitarian structure; the church bears an essential and indispensable relationship to each Person of the Trinity. However, we cannot appreciate the full measure of this insight without revisiting God's life of Trinitarian communion, for the church is to be an earthly reflection of God's eternal and Trinitarian communion. So, let us return to God.

The doctrine of the Trinity is not simply an account of God's being. Because of the incarnation of the Word, God's being is united with human nature. The doctrine of the Trinity thus has implications for how we think about human beings after the incarnation—in other words, for the doctrine of the church.

We begin with the reminder that God's Trinitarian life is a life of communion or fellowship (in Greek, *koinonia*). The divine communion is characterized by mutual love and indwelling: ". . . the Father is in me, and I in the Father" (John 10:38b). The Father and Son, therefore, are not divine beings who happen to have a relationship; on the contrary, the being of the Father and the Son is such that each exists *in* the other. The divine Persons are not beings who enter into relationship with each other; the Father, Son, and Holy Spirit *are* relations—their being consists completely in their mutual relations. The Father exists in relationship to the Son and *only* in relationship to the Son; the Son exists only in relationship to the Father. There is not Father without the Son, and no Son without the Father. The same is true of the Holy Spirit. There is, in short, nothing non-relational about the divine Persons; they are relational through and through.

This relationship of mutual indwelling explains the nature of love. To love is to be part of another being. God's life is preeminently a life of love because the Father is utterly in the Son and the Son utterly in the Father. Love thus defines God's being. We can experience this in a finite way by reflecting on the way in which our lives are joined with the lives of those whom we love: to love is to be engaged in and an integral part of the life of someone else. What is true in a fragmentary and finite way for humans is true preeminently and infinitely for Father, Son, and Spirit. So it is not that the Trinitarian Persons *have* communion with each other. Instead, they *are* communion. The life of the Persons is a life of communion; each exists only in relationship to the others.

How does all this relate to the church? We arrive at the answer by meditating on the creedal affirmation that the church is a communion of saints. God's Trinitarian life of communion is not merely fellowship between the Father and the Son in the Spirit. The communion that is God's life extends itself outward into the world, seeking to draw humankind into that communion. The history of salvation is the history of God's seeking to create communion with humankind. The creation of the church is the principal means by which God seeks to realize communion with humankind. The church is called to be the people who exist in communion with God and with other creatures. The church's mission is to invite the world into the divine communion and to actualize that communion in human community.

> Let us look once again at Jesus's prayer in John's Gospel: Holy Father, protect them by the power of your name, the name you gave me, so that they may be one as we are one.... My prayer is not for them alone. I pray also for those who will believe in me through their message, that all of them may be one, Father, just as you are in me and I am in you. May they also be in us so that the world may believe that you have sent me. I have given them the glory that you gave me, that they may be one, as we are one—I in them and you in me—so that they may be brought to complete unity. Then the world will know that you have sent me and have loved them even as you have loved me.
> (John 17:11b, 20–23)

This passage shows us that (1) the Father and Son dwell in a relationship of unity and love, and (2) they desire to extend this relationship to humankind. That is the meaning of Jesus's command to the church to love (John 13:34), and his prayer that the disciples may be united with one another (17:21). By practicing love, the disciples abide in the Father and the Son; by maintaining unity, they participate in the unity that binds Father and Son. As the church exhibits love and unity, it reproduces in human community the eternal love and unity of the Father and Son, in this way bearing witness to the world (13:35; 17:21–23). There is therefore a close connection between our relation to God and our relation to each other. As disciples love each other, they reproduce the love that exists between Father and Son. As they maintain unity with each other, they reproduce the unity that exists between Father and Son.

The Holy Spirit and Communion

As we have seen, the New Testament connects the doctrine of the church to the Holy Spirit as well as to the Father and the Son. However, the Holy Spirit has a special role to play in the church's existence as a communion. To see the Holy Spirit's role in creating the church as a communion, we need to turn to Paul's letters, which speak of the communion or fellowship (*koinonia*) of the Spirit (2 Cor. 13:13; Phil. 2:1; Heb. 6:4). Paul is speaking of the communion or fellowship the Spirit creates in the church. But these letters also present the Spirit as the principle of communion. The Holy Spirit is a divine reality in which the church participates; the Holy Spirit is not only the *principle* of *koinonia* but *is koinonia*. The early Christian theologian Augustine stated this truth forcefully by noting that the Spirit is the principle of love and unity between the Father and the Son. Accordingly, we may say that the Spirit mediates in the church the same divine love and unity that the Spirit is in the communion between the Father and the Son.

The love and unity the Spirit mediates are operative not only vertically, in the church's relation to God, but horizontally as well, in the sphere of human community. In and through the Spirit we have spiritual communion with one another; by the Spirit we are enabled to be the body of Christ with many members (1 Cor. 12:13). As a result, it is desperately important to maintain the unity of the Spirit in peace (Eph. 4:3). There may be many spirits in the world, but there is one divine, holy Spirit, and every member of Christ's body shares in this one Spirit along with every other member—hence the strong affirmation in Ephesians that, just as there is one body of Christ, so there is one Spirit (Eph. 4:4). The church is thus a communion, a sharing, and is therefore a unity.

The church's unity is based also on its status as the temple of the Holy Spirit (1 Cor. 3:16). As Paul argued, because we are the temple of the Spirit, we must take care not to destroy this temple. Paul meant that we must not do anything that would divide the church, as in fact the Corinthians had already done. Additionally, being the temple of the Spirit signifies the church's holiness: the temple was made holy by the divine presence within it. If the church is the Spirit's temple, and if the Spirit dwells within the church, then the holy presence of the Spirit sanctifies the church.

Conclusion

The church has a Trinitarian structure; it is a Trinitarian reality because, when it is true to its calling, it participates in the love, unity, and relation of communion between the Father and the Son. It does so as it allows itself to live in the power of the Holy Spirit.

Understanding the church as a Trinitarian fellowship of communion has several practical effects:

- If the church is a communion that reflects the communion between the Father and Son, then the most vital aspect of the church is the love of its members for each other and the preservation of unity. Structure and organization are important only because they promote communion.
- Renewal in the church is always a matter of strengthening love and unity.
- Thinking of the church as communion implies that each member has an active role to play in nurturing this communion, which is why Paul emphasized the importance of practicing spiritual gifts in the church.

- The church's task is to be a community of communion and to invite those outside the community to participate in its communion.
- The church as communion is more than a collection of individual people. Communion means that, just as Father and Son dwell in each other, so through the practice of love, each member of the church dwells in the others. As members of Christ's body, we are members of one another (Rom. 12:5).
- Correctly understanding the Trinity requires that we also correctly understand the nature of the church.

SEVEN — The Trinity and Worship

The Trinitarian life of God is a life of communion. This communion extends beyond the eternal being of God into communion with human beings in history. This movement occurs in the sending of the Son and then the Spirit into the world to create a community of love and unity. We can thus think of the appearance of the Trinity in history (the economic Trinity) as a movement from the Father to the Son to the Spirit. The Father sends the Son into the world. Then the Father and the Son send the Spirit into the world to establish the church. The church—insofar as it is the body of Christ and lives in the power of the Spirit—is an extension of God's Trinitarian life in history. God's Trinitarian life of communion is now embodied in the world in the church.

However, this movement (Father-Son-Spirit-church) is not a line. It is a circle because God the Father is not only the *source* of all things but also the *telos* (the goal) of all things. All things come from and return to God the Father. So, the Trinitarian life that enters into history and which constitutes the church returns to its eternal source. Everything is eschatologically destined to return to God the Father; however, in the midst of history, this return happens in a preliminary, anticipatory form. It happens in worship.

Worship is the concrete form in which creatures return to God; it is therefore the proper task of the church, for in worship the Trinitarian nature of the church expresses itself in words and deeds that are offered up to God as a sacrifice. Worship is not something we *do*; it is not a human act. On the contrary, worship is the manifestation of the triune life of God expressing itself in praise through us, who through the Spirit become willing instruments of God. God's Trinitarian life, working among us, thus evokes our response to God's communion-creating salvation, a response that takes many forms: verbal praise, practical obedience, acts of remembering and celebration, and others.

The idea that human worship is a return of divine life to God is prominent in John Wesley's writings. In his sermon "The New Birth" Wesley wrote, "God is continually breathing, as it were, upon the soul; and his soul is breathing unto God. Grace is descending into his heart; and prayer and praise ascending to heaven: And by this intercourse between God and man, this fellowship with the Father and the Son, as by a kind of spiritual respiration, the life of God in the soul is sustained."[1]

In Wesley's sermon "The Great Privilege of Those That Are Born of God" we read, "The Spirit or breath of God is immediately inspired, breathed into the new-born soul; and the same breath which comes from, returns to, God: As it is continually received by faith, so it is continually rendered back by love, by prayer, and praise, and thanksgiving; love and praise, and prayer being the breath of every soul which

---

1. John Wesley, Sermon 45, "The New Birth," II, 4, http://wesley.nnu.edu/john-wesley/the-sermons-of-john-wesley-1872-edition/sermon-45-the-new-birth/.

is truly born of God. And by this new kind of spiritual respiration, spiritual life is not only sustained, but increased day by day."[2]

These texts show us the centrality of this theme for Wesleyans. Its importance lies in the way it helps us realize that worship is not something we give to God. Instead, we should think of worship as the event in which the eternal life of God—the life of going out and return—is most fully actualized in human existence. In the act of worship, the Trinitarian life of God completes its historical movement.

The Trinitarian Structure of Worship

Let us consider a few texts that describe the church's priestly function:

- "Therefore, I urge you, brothers and sisters, in view of God's mercy, to offer your bodies as a living sacrifice, holy and pleasing to God—this is your true and proper worship" (Rom. 12:1).
- "Through Jesus, therefore, let us continually offer to God a sacrifice of praise—the fruit of lips that openly profess his name. And do not forget to do good and to share with others, for with such sacrifices God is pleased" (Heb. 13:15-16).
- "You also, like living stones, are being built into a spiritual house to be a holy priesthood, offering spiritual sacrifices acceptable to God through Jesus Christ" (1 Peter 2:5).
- "But you are a chosen people, a royal priesthood, a holy nation, God's special possession, that you may

---

2. John Wesley, Sermon 19, "The Great Privilege of Those That Are Born of God," I, 8, http://wesley.nnu.edu/john-wesley/the-sermons-of-john-wesley-1872-edition/sermon-19-the-great-privilege-of-those-that-are-born-of-god/.

declare the praises of him who called you out of darkness into his wonderful light" (1 Peter 2:9). These texts portray the church's task in the priestly role of offering sacrifice to God; however, in place of animals, the church offers spiritual sacrifices: praise and the proclamation of God's excellence, good works, and the consecration of our bodies. The church, therefore, offers something back to God. But what it offers back is simply what it has received from God, for all of the church's deeds take place in the power of the Spirit; they are all manifestations of God's Trinitarian life at work in the church. The church's sacrificial offering to God is thus the giving to God of what the church has received from God.

Next, let's consider the Trinitarian structure of *acts* of worship. Consider these texts:

- "To the only wise God be glory forever through Jesus Christ! Amen" (Rom. 16:27).
- "For through him [Christ] we both have access to the Father by one Spirit" (Eph. 2:18).
- "Always giving thanks to God the Father for everything, in the name of our Lord Jesus Christ" (Eph. 5:20).
- "And whatever you do, whether in word or deed, do it all in the name of the Lord Jesus, giving thanks to God the Father through him" (Col. 3:17).
- "But you, dear friends, by building yourselves up in your most holy faith and praying in the Holy Spirit, keep yourselves in God's love as you wait for the mercy of our Lord Jesus Christ to bring you to eternal life" (Jude 1:20–21).
- "To the only God our Savior be glory, majesty, power and authority, through Jesus Christ our Lord, before all ages, now and forevermore! Amen" (Jude 1:25).

We notice in these texts a Trinitarian structure to worship. Acts of praise, thanksgiving, etc., are directed *to* God the Father. These acts are offered to the Father *in* and *through* Jesus Christ. These acts are offered to the Father *in the power of* the Spirit. Worship, and especially prayer, are thus offered to God the Father in the name and authority of Jesus and in the power of the Spirit.

Praise is offered to God the Father because the Father is the Trinitarian Person from whom are all things (1 Cor. 8:6) and who, in the end, will be all in all (1 Cor. 15:28). All creation comes from God the Father and eventually returns to God the Father. When the church worships, it anticipates this return of all things to the Father; in worship we give all of ourselves to God the Father in anticipation of everything returning to the Father in the eschatological end. Worship is, therefore, an eschatological event—it is an appearance of the end of history in the midst of history.

Praise is offered in and through Jesus Christ because the church is the body of Christ. Its worship is not the act of a human community. On the contrary, in the act of worship, the church as the body of Christ participates in Jesus Christ's own worship of God the Father, such as when Jesus prayed that God's name might be kept holy (Matt. 6:9).

Praise is offered in the power of the Spirit because the church needs the Spirit to take its feeble words and deeds and make them acceptable to God the Father. In themselves, our prayers and other acts of worship are simply human deeds and therefore unworthy of God. The Spirit, however, consecrates these deeds and words and transforms them into acceptable sacrifices. We are thus told to pray in the Spirit (Eph. 6:18; Jude 1:20). Prayer in the Spirit, or with the Spirit's help, is necessary because "we do not know what we ought to pray for" and need the Spirit to intercede for us, to make our fallible, human words conform to God's will (Rom. 8:26,

27). For the same reason, we are also to worship in the Spirit (John 4:23–24; Phil. 3:3). Even our confession of faith happens with the power of the Spirit: "no one can say, 'Jesus is Lord,' except by the Holy Spirit (1 Cor. 12:3b).

Worship, therefore, has a Trinitarian structure. To worship God the Father in and through Jesus Christ and in the power of the Spirit is to practice the doctrine of the Trinity. While we often think of theological doctrines as consisting of truths that we are to believe, doctrines are also truths that are to be practiced. When the church offers authentic worship, it is participating in the Trinitarian life of God. It is, in a sense, enacting or performing the doctrine of the Trinity.

The Trinitarian Structure of the Lord's Supper

The Lord's Supper is the principal means by which the church realizes its status as a community of communion. Consider these passages:

- Those who eat Christ's flesh and drink his blood abide in him, and he abides in them (John 6:56).
- The cup that we bless is a sharing (*koinonia*) in the blood of Christ. The bread that we break is a sharing (*koinonia*) in the body of Christ. Since there is one bread, we who are many are one body (1 Cor. 10:16–17).

These two texts show us that the Lord's Supper accomplishes our communion with God and with each other. By our participation in the Lord's Supper we abide in Jesus. We share in his body and blood, and we are made to be one communal body, having communion with one another. Because the Lord's Supper is the preeminent event in which the church realizes its nature as communion, John Wesley urged us to celebrate the Supper as frequently as possible.[3] As an act of communion, the Lord's Supper is the church's collective participation in the life of God, which is a life of eternal communion.

The creation of communion is the fundamental meaning of the Lord's Supper; however, it has other aspects, and they too exhibit an overtly Trinitarian structure. The Supper is an act of thanksgiving (in Greek, *eucharistia*) to God the Father, in remembrance of Jesus Christ, in the communion (*koinonia*) of the Spirit.

The Lord's Supper is an act of giving thanks to God (Matt. 26:26, 27; Mark 14:22, 23; Luke 22:19). This is an aspect of the church's priestly task of offering to God spiritual sacrifices of praise. Like all prayers, thanksgiving is directed to God the Father.

The Supper is also an act of remembrance (Luke 22:19) and proclamation (1 Cor. 11:26). In it we look back to Jesus and his death, and we also look forward to his coming. In liturgical churches, the portion of the liturgy devoted to remembrance is called the *anamnesis*, the Greek word for remembering.

The Supper requires the Spirit's act of sanctification. Unfortunately, many evangelical and Wesleyan churches have given little thought to this aspect of the Lord's Supper; other churches have considered it carefully. In The Book of Common Prayer, for example, one prays that God may "cleanse the thoughts of our hearts by the inspiration of your Holy Spirit, that we may perfectly love you, and worthily magnify your holy Name," and asks God to "sanctify [the bread and cup] by your Holy Spirit to be for your people the

---

3. See John Wesley, Sermon 101, "The Duty of Constant Communion," http://wesley.nnu.edu/john-wesley/the-sermons-of-john-wesley-1872-edition/sermon-101-the-duty-of-constant-communion/.

Body and Blood of your Son, the holy food and drink of new and unending life in him. Sanctify us also that we may faithfully receive this holy Sacrament."[4] Catholic and Orthodox churches use the term *epiclesis* to indicate the prayer for the Spirit to come upon the bread and cup. The Spirit's sanctification causes the bread and cup to become sacramental elements that mediate God's grace. The Spirit also prepares us to sacramentally receive the elements.

This sanctifying aspect of the Holy Spirit's work is important for every part of worship, which is why every worship service should include a prayer of invocation, where we call upon the Father to send the Spirit of Christ, sanctifying the time and place of worship as well as the worshipers. We need the sanctifying work of the Spirit to enable us to hear the Bible as the Word of God and to hear God speaking to us in the preaching of the Word.

The Trinitarian Structure of Baptism

Christian baptism has the most obvious Trinitarian structure imaginable. It is performed in the name of the triune God as Jesus instructed in Matthew 28:19; however, its Trinitarian structure rests on more than simply its liturgical expression.

Baptism has a strongly christological character. Jesus is the agent of baptism—he baptizes with the Holy Spirit (Mark 1:8). That is why, in Acts, baptism is performed in the name of Jesus (2:38)—it is *his* baptism; those who baptize are merely Christ's instruments. Additionally, baptism is the event in which we die and are buried with Christ (Rom. 6:3–4; Col. 2:12); and, through the resurrection of Christ, baptism saves us (1 Peter 3:21).

---

4. The (Online) Book of Common Prayer," The Holy Eucharist: Rite Two, http://bcponline.org.

At the same time, baptism is also a pneumatological event. There is an obvious connection; baptism seems to be a prerequisite for receiving the Spirit (Acts 2:38), although sometimes the Spirit is received before baptism (Acts 10:47). Beyond this obvious connection, we learn that baptism brings rebirth and the Spirit's renewal (Titus 3:5; John 3:5). The Holy Spirit is the spiritual medium, corresponding to physical water, in which we are baptized—that is why the New Testament speaks of our being baptized in or with the Spirit. But the Spirit is more than just the medium in which we are baptized; according to Paul, the Spirit baptizes us into the one body of Christ (1 Cor. 12:13) and into Jesus Christ (Gal. 3:27). The Spirit is thus as much the agent of baptism as is Jesus Christ.

The connection between baptism and God the Father is seen in the fact that baptism is the means by which we are incorporated into the holy nation and royal priesthood whose task it is to render spiritual worship to God the Father.

Concluding Thoughts

It is important to recognize and emphasize the Trinitarian nature of worship. Without this acknowledgment, the worshiping community becomes not a communion but a collection of individuals who come together because of shared interests—like any other association. Without this emphasis, the act of worship becomes something we *do*, instead of being an act in which we participate in God's Trinitarian life. That is why the doctrine of the Trinity is not so much an article of faith to be believed as a doctrine to be practiced. Like acts of love, worship is the performance of the doctrine of the Trinity.

EIGHT — The Trinity and the Church's Holiness

The theme of this chapter is the holiness of the church and the Trinitarian structure of that holiness. This theme is worthy of attention because it is routinely ignored in discussions about Christian holiness. In such discussions, the sole focus of attention is usually the holy character and behavior of individual disciples. Such character and behavior are, of course, of paramount importance; at the same time, it is curious that the church's corporate holiness is almost never considered, given its prominence in the Bible and its significance for the doctrine of Christian holiness.

Both the Apostles' Creed and the Nicene Creed affirm belief in the holy church. What does it mean to believe in a holy church? The church's holiness must be more than the aggregate holiness of its members; no amount of individual holiness could ever justify making the holiness of the church an article of faith. So, while it is vital for individual members to be and act holy, the church's corporate holiness does not rest on the holiness of its members. Its holiness must be sought in its relation to the triune God.

Holiness and Election

It is commonly understood that holiness is a matter of separation. But what do we mean by separation? To answer this question, it is instructive to look at Israel, for the church is the continuation of Israel—the holy people of God.

From the perspective of the Old Testament, Israel exists only because of an act of divine election: God created Israel as a people by an act of choice, or election, and thus constituted Israel as a separated people, distinct from their neighbors. Election was God's act of calling Israel to be God's own people. In this act of election, Israel was separated from the nations and devoted to God's exclusive possession and use. This act of separation through election constituted Israel as a holy people: "For you are a people holy to the Lord your God. The Lord your God has chosen you out of all the peoples on the face of the earth to be his people, his treasured possession" (Deut. 7:6). Israel possessed corporate holiness; it was a holy people.

This corporate holiness was more than the collective holiness of its members. Within the community of Israel, certain people—the priests—enjoyed holy status because of their priestly role. Others—notably those who undertook the Nazirite vow—became holy through special practices. But over and above such individuals, Israel as a people was holy. Its corporate holiness was the result of God's election. By choosing Israel to be God's special people, by thus distinguishing Israel from the other nations, God constituted Israel as a holy people.

In this context, "holy" does not refer to any special moral or spiritual quality; it refers instead to Israel's *status* as a people who belong to God in a special way. Of course, individual Israelites were obliged to respond to God's call by acting in ways consistent with Israel's corporate holiness.

This is the lesson of Leviticus 19, which calls upon Israelites to actualize their status as holy people through concrete acts of moral behavior. However, even when Israelites failed to act consistently within their holy status—and even when their behavior contradicted that status—Israel as a corporate entity was still, from God's perspective, everlastingly chosen and, hence, holy. This understanding of holiness explains how inanimate objects can be regarded as holy in the Old Testament. Utensils in the temple, animals for sacrifice, and the temple itself were holy—not because of any spiritual or moral quality but because they had been consecrated to God. They became God's possession. Their holiness, like that of Israel collectively, was a matter of status.

In the New Testament, this understanding of Israel's holiness transfers to the church. The clearest New Testament witness to this truth is 1 Peter 2:9a: "But you are a chosen people, a royal priesthood, a holy nation, God's special possession." These same words describe Israel in Exodus 19:6. The church is a holy people just as Israel was a holy people. The church possesses holiness because it is the people of God who have been separated from the world by an act of divine election, just as Israel was elected, separated, and rendered holy. Its holiness rests on its status in relation to God, not on the combined holiness of its individual members.

Incidentally, the Bible's teaching about election contains an important corrective. The doctrine of election is often reduced to the idea of predestination, which in turn is almost always interpreted in exclusively individual terms. In other words, the doctrine of election and predestination are taken to mean God's seemingly arbitrary selection of individuals for salvation and the rejection of others. Biblical texts such as those mentioned in this chapter remind us that the object of election is a corporate body—Israel in the

Old Testament, the church in the New Testament. Israel and the church, considered as corporate bodies, are the elect. Understanding election in this way ensures that we do not interpret it individualistically, as the doctrine of predestination is usually presented.

The Trinitarian Basis of Election

Several biblical texts give us the Trinitarian basis for divine election:

- "For he [God] chose us in him [Christ] before the creation of the world to be holy and blameless in his sight. In love he predestined us for adoption to sonship through Jesus Christ, in accordance with his pleasure and will" (Eph. 1:4–5).
- "For we know, brothers and sisters loved by God, that he has chosen you, because our gospel came to you not simply with words but also with power, with the Holy Spirit and deep conviction" (1 Thess. 1:4–5a).
- "But we ought always to thank God for you, brothers and sisters loved by the Lord, because God chose you as firstfruits to be saved through the sanctifying work of the Spirit and through belief in the truth. He called you to this through our gospel, that you might share in the glory of our Lord Jesus Christ" (2 Thess. 2:13–14).
- "To God's elect . . . who have been chosen according to the foreknowledge of God the Father, through the sanctifying work of the Spirit, to be obedient to Jesus Christ and sprinkled with his blood" (1 Peter 1:1b, 2a).

Passages such as these show us that God's act of electing a holy people, like all of God's acts, has a Trinitarian structure. God the Father calls, elects, and separates. The church's corporate holiness is ultimately grounded in God

The potential tension between holy status and holy character explains why the New Testament frequently asserts that the church must be a pure people, purified by God.

the Father's election. God the Father elects the church in Jesus Christ, just as God creates in Christ. And election is actualized by the sanctifying work of the Holy Spirit. The call of God thus comes from the Trinity and expresses God's Trinitarian life.

Further Thoughts on Corporate Holiness

The New Testament regards the church as a corporate entity and not as a collection of individuals. Of course, the church has members who are particular people; it is not an abstraction. Nonetheless, we cannot make sense of the New Testament's teaching about the church unless we recognize the church's corporate character. This is why the New Testament's central metaphors for the church—household of God, spouse of Christ, temple of the Spirit, and body of Christ—are so important; they are constant reminders of the church's corporate existence.

The corporate character of the church is important for many theological and pastoral reasons; one of those reasons is that it helps us understand the New Testament's teaching about holiness. In an individualistic society—for example, industrial-technological cultures—it is natural to think of holiness in terms of individual piety and behavior. But for the New Testament, holiness is first a matter of participating in the holy people of God—the body that has been elected and set apart by God. This means that the church has a holiness that transcends the holiness of its members. Before disciples individually attain a holy character, they possess a holy status as members of Christ's body, the church.

It is crucial that we understand the distinction between holiness of character and holiness as status: Israel's status as the holy people did not mean every Israelite possessed a holy character and acted in accordance with holiness. At times, individuals in Israel acted in distinctly unholy ways, especially when they failed to maintain separation from the surrounding nations. Nonetheless, they were still part of the holy, elect, separate people.

This distinction between holiness of character and holy status explains Paul's remarks to the Corinthians. He called the Corinthians saints (i.e., "holy ones") and noted twice that they had been sanctified (1 Cor. 1:2; 6:11); however, their conduct was anything but holy. In response, Paul repeatedly exhorted them to reconcile their unholy conduct with their holy status as a separated people—to walk worthy of their calling as a holy, separate people (2 Cor. 6:17). There was a contradiction between their status as members of the holy people (the church) and their conduct as individuals. Because of this distinction, Paul could truly affirm their holy status as members of the elect people of God while demanding the holy conduct and character they lacked.

The potential tension between holy status and holy character explains why the New Testament frequently asserts that the church must be a pure people, purified by God (Eph. 5:25–27), preserving itself from defilement by the world (2 Cor. 7:1), and holy in its conduct (1 Peter 1:15). Purity and holiness become a task to be actualized in conduct, a task that presumes the church's status as the holy people.

The Church and the Holy Life

Apart from the corporate meaning of holiness, the church as a corporate entity is important for holiness in another sense. The church is the context that prepares us to hear the call of God and in which—through preaching, teaching, sacraments, and example—God awakens us and calls us to repentance. As the temple and house of the Spirit, it is the place where consecration is nurtured, where Christian character is developed, and where love is taught and exemplified.

The church is the means God uses to call us and to elicit a faithful response. In other words, the church is a means of grace and thus has a sacramental function. In the sacraments, God uses human acts—such as giving, receiving, and eating food—to convey grace to us. In them, divine action is joined to human action. What is particularly true of the sacraments is true of the church generally. In its ministries, both formal and informal, God leads us into the holy life. For instance, one may hear God's call through a formal ministry of the church (such as preaching or education) or through an informal ministry (such as the example of a holy life). Accordingly, the path to holiness is found in the church and its influence on us. That is why our relationship with God depends on our membership in the community of the church.

John Wesley's theology presents a particularly strong resource for thinking about the importance of Christian community for holiness. Wesley was convinced of the importance of the church's outward means of grace. In part, this is accounted for by his high-church upbringing. But part of it is explained by his keen sense of the actual ways people come to be holy. From observation he knew the church's means of grace are vital.

What sorts of things did Wesley include as means of grace? He meant the two sacraments (baptism and the Lord's Supper) but also many other Christian practices as well: prayer of all sorts (private prayer, family prayer, and public prayer) and searching the Scriptures (studying, meditating, and putting their truths into practice). Other practices included fasting, mutual counsel, regular meetings with other Christians for growth and accountability, the arts of holy living, and self-discipline in physical pleasures.

However, it is vital that we remember the holy life is more than holy character and conduct. It is, in essence, a participation in the Trinitarian life of God, which is a life of communion. It is easy to forget this point, for sanctification is becoming like God. This process is often referred to as *theosis* in Greek or *deification* in Latin. Consider these texts:

- Lev. 19:2: We are to be holy as God is holy.
- Matt. 5:48: We are to be perfect as our heavenly Father is perfect.
- Eph. 5:1: We are to be imitators of God.

However, if we pay attention *only* to texts like these, we will misunderstand the nature of holiness, for we will think of holiness simply as imitating God. Although we *should* seek to be like God, it is also important to remember the participatory nature of holiness and to recall that "it is God who works in you to will and to act in order to fulfill his good purpose" (Phil. 2:13). "I no longer live, but Christ lives in me" (Gal. 2:20). The imitation of God is not something *we* do; it is something *God* does *in* us as we abide in God—as we participate in God's Trinitarian life.

To gain an appropriate view of God—and, therefore, of Christian holiness—we should meditate on a text such as 2 Peter 1:4 which declares we are partakers of the divine nature. It tells us that God's being is such that, as Jesus's disciples, we can share in that being. John affirms that we abide in God (John 15:4) and that those who abide in love abide in God (1 John 4:16). Such abiding in God is possible only because God *is* love (1 John 4:8). Because love is communion, God's being, which is love, is communion and is therefore a reality in which we can share. Holiness, therefore, is love because it is the perfection of our participation in God, whose life is a life of love and communion. The life of holiness is a life in which the Trinity lives in us and leads us into acts of love and communion. This is the Trinitarian basis on which holiness of character and conduct is founded.

NINE: The Trinity and the Spiritual Gifts

It may seem strange for a book about the Trinity to have a chapter on the spiritual gifts, but it is not at all strange once we see that the gifts are manifestations of Christ's gifts administered through the Holy Spirit for the common good of the church (1 Cor. 12:7). The concept of spiritual gifts is an integral part of ecclesiology (the doctrine of the church). And, as we have seen, the church has a Trinitarian structure. As the body of Christ, the temple of the Spirit, and the royal priesthood offering spiritual sacrifices to God the Father, the church is a Trinitarian reality. It is the extension of God's Trinitarian life into history, a community that participates in the Trinitarian movement of coming forth and returning. As is true of all the other topics covered in Christian theology, a full understanding of spiritual gifts requires seeing their Trinitarian basis and structure.

Think about these passages:
- "For just as each of us has one body with many members, and these members do not all have the same function, so in Christ we, though many, form one body, and each member belongs to all the oth-

ers. We have different gifts, according to the grace given to each of us" (Rom. 12:4–6a).

- "There are different kinds of gifts, but the same Spirit distributes them. There are different kinds of service, but the same Lord. There are different kinds of working, but in all of them and in everyone it is the same God at work. Now to each one the manifestation of the Spirit is given for the common good" (1 Cor. 12:4–7).

- "But to each one of us grace has been given as Christ apportioned it. So Christ himself gave the apostles, the prophets, the evangelists, the pastors and teachers" (Eph. 4:7, 11).

- "Each of you should use whatever gift you have received to serve others, as faithful stewards of God's grace in its various forms. If anyone speaks, they should do so as one who speaks the very words of God. If anyone serves, they should do so with the strength God provides, so that in all things God may be praised through Jesus Christ. To him be the glory and the power for ever and ever. Amen" (1 Peter 4:10–11).

Passages such as these show us that each member of the Trinity is involved in the spiritual gifts; they are a work of the entire Trinity. They are grounded in God the Father, for they are forms of God's grace; they have a christological basis, for they are functions of the entire body of Christ, the church; and they are pneumatological realities—manifestations of the Spirit. Therefore, it is proper to study the gifts not exclusively as part of the doctrine of the Holy Spirit but as a consequence of God's Trinitarian life.

Nonetheless, there is a special connection between the gifts and the Spirit that reaches back into the Old Testament. The connection lies in the fact that the Spirit is the principle of life. In Genesis 2, the breath (*neshamah*) of God transforms dust into a living being; in Genesis 1, the divine Spirit (*ruah*) hovers over the primordial water, preparing it for the action of God's creative word. The Spirit is the divine agency that transforms creation into something extraordinary. The Spirit is, consequently, specially associated with the new creation.

Prophetic Inspiration in the Old Testament

The Spirit that creates life also creates the prophetic word. As 2 Peter 1 indicates, prophecy is not a result of human will but instead occurs as humans are moved by the Holy Spirit (vv. 20-21). We see this principle in Numbers 11: "Then the Lord came down in the cloud and spoke with him, and he took some of the power of the Spirit that was on him [Moses] and put it on the seventy elders. When the Spirit rested on them, they prophesied—but did not do so again" (v. 25). The simple presence of the Spirit, it seems, was enough to inspire the elders to prophesy. This means that the prophetic word is, in a special sense, God's word; it is the effect of God's Spirit.

Numerous scriptures tell us that, when the prophets spoke, it was God speaking through them by the Spirit (Neh. 9:30; Zech. 7:12; 1 Pet. 1:10-12). Deuteronomy 18:18 goes so far as to say that God will put the divine word into the mouth of the prophet who will be like Moses. This is why Paul told us to respect the words of the prophets (1 Thess. 5:20), for they are God's speech to us. Of course, the Bible also tells us to scrutinize prophetic declarations, including Paul in the very next verse (1 Thess. 5:21; see also 1 Cor. 14:29)—for not everyone who claims to be a prophet was sent by God.

Spirit possession often led the prophets into unusual experiences. One of the outstanding examples is Saul in

1 Samuel 19.[1] While Saul was seeking David, the Spirit of God fell on him, and he began "prophesying" (vv. 23-24). What did it mean for Saul to prophesy? We get a wrong picture if we imagine that Saul delivered a public speech akin to Jeremiah or Isaiah. Instead, we have to look at episodes such as 1 Samuel 18:10, where Saul began prophesying in the presence of David and flew into a manic rage, or 1 Kings 18:28-29, where the prophets of Baal "prophesied" all day long, which involved crying out repeatedly and cutting themselves. In these contexts, prophecy is not a public speech but is instead a strange experience with frenzied behavior. In 1 Samuel 19, when Saul prophesied, he stripped off his clothes and lay naked for an entire day and night. It's no wonder that prophets in this period were sometimes regarded as crazy (see 2 Kings 9:1-11, esp. v. 11).

Even prophets whom we regard as more "mainstream" had highly unusual experiences of Spirit possession. Consider Ezekiel's experience:

> Then the spirit lifted me up, and as the glory of the LORD rose from its place, I heard behind me the sound of loud rumbling; it was the sound of the wings of the living creatures brushing against one another, and the sound of the wheels beside them, that sounded like a loud rumbling. The spirit lifted me up and bore me away; I went in bitterness in the heat of my spirit, the hand of the LORD being strong upon me. (Ezek. 3:12-14, NRSV).

It is thus not surprising that John had a vision of the risen Jesus and of heaven while he was "in the Spirit" (Rev. 1:10-16; 4:1-2).

---

1. Instances of "spirit possession" don't always involve the Holy Spirit. In Saul's case, the reference is to ecstatic behavior, specifically ecstatic dancing.

At the same time, to keep things in perspective, it is good to remember that extraordinary experiences were not exactly the norm in the prophetic tradition. There is no indication of such experiences in Hosea's prophetic career; the closest that Amos came was receiving the word of God as he experienced ordinary things—locusts (7:1) and a basket of fruit (8:1).

Extraordinary Gifts in the Old Testament

We can think of inspiration as the act of empowering the prophet to speak God's word. But the Spirit's empowerment took other forms in the Old Testament. Israel's judges (who were really war leaders) led after they received the Spirit (Judg. 3:9–10; 6:34; 11:29). Other great leaders, such as Joshua (Num. 27:18) and David (1 Sam. 16:13) owed their greatness to the Spirit.

More unusual than the Spirit's empowerment for leadership is the case of Samson. In his case, Spirit possession showed itself mainly in his capacity for mayhem: killing a lion (Judg. 14:6), killing thirty Philistines (Judg. 14:19), and breaking his bonds, enabling him to kill more Philistines (Judg. 15:14).

A less violent effect of Spirit possession is found in people like Joseph and Daniel. From the Spirit they received extraordinary wisdom and understanding (Gen. 41:38–39; Dan. 5:11). Even an everyday skill like woodworking could be regarded as Spirit-inspired, as when Moses needed someone to work on the tabernacle (Exod. 35:30).

The Holy Spirit's Inspiration in the New Testament

Just as in the Old Testament, the Holy Spirit is the Spirit of prophecy in the New Testament. Several New Testament passages show us that prophecy was an important part of the early church:

- The Christian prophet Agabus, in the Spirit, predicted a famine (Acts 11:28).
- Agabus also prophesied according to the Holy Spirit that Paul would be bound if he went to Jerusalem (Acts 21:10–11).
- "The Spirit clearly says that in later times some will abandon the faith and follow deceiving spirits and things taught by demons" (1 Tim. 4:1). This verse is reporting a prophecy, not quoting a biblical text.
- Revelation seven times warns the reader to listen to what the Spirit says to the seven churches (Rev. 2:7, 11, 17, 29; 3:6, 13, 22).

These passages and others make it clear there were Christian prophets in the early church; the church accepted their oracles as utterances of the Holy Spirit. As we will see, the early church had good reason to be cautious about prophetic declarations. Nonetheless, Spirit-inspired prophecy was an accepted part of early Christianity.

Besides inspiring prophecy, the New Testament tells us the Spirit guided the thoughts and actions of early Christians. The Spirit, for instance, prompted Philip to approach the Ethiopian (Acts 8:29), directed Peter to receive Cornelius's delegation (Acts 10:19) and to accompany them back to Cornelius (Acts 11:12), told the church to consecrate Barnabas and Paul for missionary service (Acts 13:2), guided the choice of Paul's mission fields (Acts 16:6–7), and testified to Paul that he would be persecuted (Acts 20:23). Curiously, when it became evident that Paul would face troubles in Jerusalem, his companions urged him through the Spirit not to go to Jerusalem (Acts 21:4). Both Paul's determination to go and his companions' counsel not to go were inspired by the Holy Spirit.

The Holy Spirit's Illumination in the New Testament

Along with this sort of guidance, the Holy Spirit was experienced in the New Testament churches as a source of enlightenment and understanding. John's Gospel is especially important in this regard. The Spirit is called the Spirit of truth, abiding in the disciples (14:17). The Spirit's principal task is to teach the disciples and bring the words of Jesus to mind (14:26), to guide the disciples, and to declare to them the things to come (15:26). This is probably the meaning of the affirmation in 1 John 2 that "you have an anointing from the Holy One, and all of you know the truth" (v. 20; see also v. 27). Of course, the Spirit's role in teaching does not rule out the need for human teachers. Otherwise, neither John's Gospel nor 1 John would have been necessary. Still, these passages point to a central early Christian belief that the ultimate guide to truth is the Holy Spirit.

This conviction lies behind the prayer in Ephesians 1 for disciples to receive the Spirit of wisdom and revelation with enlightened hearts (v. 17), as well as the prayer in Ephesians 3 that, being strengthened with power through the Holy Spirit, we might comprehend God's love (vv. 16–18). Paul's confidence that the Spirit provides wisdom explains his freedom to write authoritatively about marriage in the absence of a specific teaching on the subject by Jesus (1 Cor. 7:12, 39–40).

Most important in this regard is Paul's teaching in 1 Corinthians that the revelation of God in Jesus Christ can be understood only by the Spirit's illumination (2:10). Having received God's Spirit, we understand what God has given to us; we speak with words learned not from human wisdom but from the Spirit (vv. 12–13). Without the Spirit, people are not able to understand the things of the Spirit. Indeed, they seem foolish (v. 14).

The Holy Spirit, then, not only inspires prophetic speech but also provides disciples with wisdom and understanding.

The Holy Spirit's Empowerment in the New Testament

As in the Old Testament, so in the New Testament the Holy Spirit empowers people to accomplish God's will. Under the influence of the Spirit in the book of Acts, Christians spoke with boldness (4:31), had visions (7:55), imposed curses (13:9–11), and prophesied and spoke in other tongues (19:6).

Spirit and power, in fact, are closely linked in Paul's letters. His discourse among the Corinthians was a "demonstration of the Spirit's power" (1 Cor. 2:4), and the preached word came to the Thessalonians in power and in the Spirit (1 Thess. 1:5). He could thus summarize his ministry as occurring in the Spirit's power (Rom. 15:19).

The Gifts of the Spirit

The Gospels record a close relationship between Jesus and the Holy Spirit throughout Jesus's earthly ministry.

According to Matthew, the Spirit led Jesus into the wilderness, where he was tempted (4:1). Jesus also cast out demons in the power of the Spirit (12:28).

Mark says the Holy Spirit descended upon Jesus at the time of his baptism and then sent him into the desert, where Satan tempted him (1:10–12).

According to Luke, the Holy Spirit is particularly influential in Jesus's ministry. The Virgin Mary conceived Jesus by the power of the Holy Spirit (1:35). After Jesus's baptism, during which the Spirit descended on him (3:22), he returned from the Jordan "full of the Holy Spirit" (4:1). Following his temptation in the wilderness, Jesus returned to Galilee "in the power of the Spirit" (4:14), and the Holy Spirit anointed him as he preached his first sermon (4:18). Jesus promised to give the Holy Spirit in abundance "to those who ask" (11:13).

In the Gospel of John, John the Baptist testified that he "saw the Spirit come down from heaven as a dove and remain" upon Jesus at his baptism (1:32). Jesus told Nicodemus that the new birth comes through the Holy Spirit (3:5–8). And he repeatedly promised the Holy Spirit to those who believe in him (7:38–39; 14:15–17; 15:26; 16:13).

Paul's teaching about the gifts of the Spirit is exceedingly important for the church's existence as the body of Christ. As a body, the church has members with differing functions (Rom. 12:4–8), all of which are vital (1 Cor. 12:14–27). The gifts differ in specific function, but they all have the same threefold purpose: (1) the perfecting of the saints; (2) the work of ministry; and (3) building up the body of Christ (Eph. 4:11–12). That is why Paul repeatedly emphasized that the Spirit distributes the gifts for the common good and building up of the church (1 Cor. 12:7; 14:5, 12, 17–19, 26).

What are the gifts? They are manifestations of the Spirit, riches procured by Christ in his atonement and ascension to the Father (Eph. 4:7–9). They are ways in which the Spirit of God appears in the people of God (1 Cor. 12:7). We should not think that the gifts are one thing and the Spirit another. Rather, the gifts are ways in which the Spirit of God appears in the church, moving God's people to act on behalf of the body of Christ in works of power and inspiration. The gifts are the way that the Spirit ensures the well-being of Christ's church. This is such a vital point that it really becomes a criterion: nothing can be accepted as a spiritual gift unless it genuinely and directly perfects the saints, aids in the work of ministry, and builds up the body of Christ.

We will revisit the gifts of the Spirit in chapter 11 as we look at them as eschatological gifts and signs of the presence of the kingdom of God.

The Trinity and the Church's Mission

Within the church one often hears that the church has a mission—that it is called to proclaim the gospel to the world. We often think of the church's mission in connection with Matthew 28:19–20: "Therefore go and make disciples of all nations, baptizing them in the name of the Father and of the Son and of the Holy Spirit, and teaching them to obey everything I have commanded you. And surely I am with you always, to the very end of the age." This is a powerful text and is important for connecting the church's mission to the Trinity; however, there is another, lesser known passage in which Jesus commissions the disciples, John 20:21: "Again Jesus said, 'Peace be with you! As the Father has sent me, I am sending you.'" John's version of the Commission highlights the connection between mission and sending. To grasp this connection, it is helpful to remember that the word "mission" comes from the Latin verb *mitto*, meaning "to send;" ergo, mission involves sending.

The Trinitarian Structure of the Church's Mission

John 20:21 does more than connect the church's mission to sending. It also expresses a more important truth not found in Matthew's Gospel—namely, that the sending of the church into the world is a continuation of—an extension of—the Father's sending of the Son into the world and the subsequent sending of the Holy Spirit. John's Gospel has an emphatic sequence of sendings: the Father sends the Son (7:28, among several others); upon returning to heaven, Jesus sends the Spirit (15:26; John's Gospel adds in 14:26 that the Father will send the Spirit in Jesus's name); finally, Jesus sends the disciples into the world (17:18; 20:21). This sequence of sendings—of missions—portrays the progressive movement of God into the world, first in the incarnate Word and then in the Spirit-inspired community. It is, accordingly, God who has a mission, reflected in the sending of the Son and the Spirit; the church exists as the community that, in the power of the Spirit, continues God's missional movement in the world.

Thinking of the church's mission in the world in terms of John's Gospel (in addition to Matthew's Gospel) places the church's mission in a Trinitarian framework. It tells us that the church's going into the world is part of God's movement into the world; it is a step in the sequence of divine sendings. Before the church even existed, God already undertook a mission into the world in the sending of the Son. So, when the church goes into the world to offer testimony, it is participating in the Trinitarian movement of God into the world. The church goes into the world as the body of Christ and in the power of the Spirit. The church is, in a sense, an extension of God's Trinitarian movement;

it is the presence of God's Trinitarian life of communion in the world.

The communal character of God's Trinitarian being tells of something very important about the church. God's Trinitarian life is a community—a life of communion (*koinonia*)—hence the numerous passages in John's Gospel affirming that the Father and the Son mutually dwell in each other. Because the church's mission is an extension of and participation in God's Trinitarian mission, the church should be a model of God's outgoing communion. The church is to be a community of communion—of *koinonia*. This truth implies that the church should not be an enclosed, inward-looking and exclusive community but instead should be an outward-looking, inclusive community. To put the matter differently: as noted earlier, the movement of God into the world is not linear but circular; this movement gathers up all things in creation and returns them to God the Father so that, in Paul's words, God may be all in all. God's mission thus aims at gathering up all things in Christ (Eph. 1:10) and reconciling all things to God (Col. 1:20). This mission becomes historically concrete in the creation and sending of the church as a community of communion.

What does it look like to be a community of Trinitarian communion? For one thing, it means being a community of love and unity, as set forth in John 17—to be a community that mirrors the love and unity that subsist between the Father and the Son. It means to be a community in which each member lives in and through the others, just as the Father is in the Son and the Son is in the Father. In terms drawn from Paul's theology, it means existing as members of a body such that "if one part suffers, every part suffers with it; if one part is honored, every part rejoices with it" (1 Cor. 12:26).

Being a community of communion also means being a community of reconciliation. In the first century, the pressing task was the reconciliation of Jews and gentiles into one body, the church (see Eph. 2). More broadly, Paul sought the reconciliation of slaves and free, and men and women as well (Gal. 3:28). Colossians even envisions the reconciliation of all things in Jesus Christ (Col. 1:19–20). In order, then, for the church to be a Trinitarian community of communion, it must get rid of the beliefs and practices that are operative in the world—beliefs and practices that separate people. The church should be characterized by reconciliation, not by separation. Only then can the church realize its nature as a community of communion.

The Trinitarian structure of the church's mission—the commission that it be an outward-moving, inclusive community of communion—raises the issue of sectarianism and separation. Because the church is holy, it is called to separate from the world. At the same time, in attempting to enact a proper separation, the church faces the temptation to make itself uninviting and to erect firm barriers between those inside and those outside. When it does this, it contradicts its nature as a Trinitarian community of communion. The church must simultaneously practice separation from the world while also being open and inviting to those who are in the world. In this delicate and tense demand, the church must follow the example of the incarnate Word, who was free of sin but also existed in complete identity with humankind—a fact seen in his association with tax collectors and sinners (Luke 7:36–50; 19:1–10).

In the tension between separation from the world's sin and being an inviting, reconciling community, the church should err on the side of reconciliation. The church is called to be pure and separate from the world, but the idea of a pure people exists *alongside* the idea of the church as a spiritual hospital. As a hospital, it is filled with sick people who are slowly regaining health. The church should therefore deal gently and patiently with people and their failings. The church should be a house of grace, where broken and damaged people can find God's healing salvation incarnated in a loving, accepting community.

Finally, let us consider John 13:35: "By this everyone will know that you are my disciples, if you love one another." Here the Gospel connects the church's witness (15:27) with its status as the community of love. The church is called to bear witness to God, but what forms does this witness take? Undoubtedly there are many forms, but the principal form of testimony is the love found within the church because God is love and because the church participates in the love and unity that subsist between the Father and the Son. Although verbal testimony is important, John's Gospel suggests that more important is the church realizing its nature as the community of communion, love, reconciliation, and unity. When the church practices love, it shows forth the God who is love.

In this way the church differs from the world. In the world there is separation and discrimination; in the church there is unity and equality. In the world there is anger and hatred; in the church there should be love and communion. To the extent that the church—through the Spirit—can actualize this communion, love, unity, and reconciliation, it will stand apart from the world. In doing so, it will offer testimony to the world that God is in fact love.

Mission and the Trinitarian Life of God

Thinking of the church's mission in this way tells us something important not only about the church but also about the eternal Trinity. Theologians long ago noted that there is an important connection between, on one hand, the sequence of sending (the Father sends the Son; Father and Son send the Spirit) and, on the other hand, the relationships among the Trinitarian Persons in eternity. To use the traditional terminology, in the eternal life of God, the Son eternally proceeds from the Father in an act of begetting (or generation). The Spirit then proceeds from the Father (and, in Western Christianity, from the Son).

Observe that the order of sending in history corresponds to the order of generation and procession in eternity. In eternity (1) the Father eternally begets or generates the Son; in history the Father sends the Son into the world. In eternity (2) the Father and Son eternally breathe forth the Spirit; in history the Father and Son send the Spirit into the world. The correspondence between the acts of sending in history and the acts of proceeding in eternity tells us that God's eternal Trinitarian life is a life of movement—of generation and procession. Mission and movement characterize not only God's appearance in history—the economic Trinity—but also God's eternal life. God's eternal being is a living movement, a life that is expansive and outgoing. God is not a unitary being, enclosed within Godself and hidden from what lies outside. On the contrary, God's life is inherently expansive; God's life is eternally opened up in a Trinitarian movement.

This expansiveness is why early Christians sometimes used the analogy of a fountain or the sun to describe the Trinity. A fountain and the sun are examples of finite realities from which something (water or light) flows forth; they involve movement. These analogies illustrate the nature of God's Trinitarian life as a life that expresses itself outwardly. From the depths of God's infinite being, the Son eternally flows forth from God the Father; from the Father through the Son, the Spirit is eternally breathed out.

But the outward movement of God does not terminate with the Son and the Spirit. The eternal God also creates a world. The creation of the world, although a free act of God, is continuous with the outward movement of God's life. The creation of a world is not only consistent with God's nature but is also a logical result of God's nature. If God is eternally a life of Trinitarian movement—of going out from the Father, through the Son, in the Spirit—then we are not surprised that God would reflect this outward Trinitarian movement in a free act that parallels the generation of the Son and the procession of the Spirit. This free act is creation. And, having created the world, the outward movement of God's Trinitarian life spills over into the world in sending the Son and the Spirit, and in creating the church.

God's being is not enclosed and hidden. On the contrary, it is expansive and outgoing. It goes out of itself, first in the procession of the Son and Spirit, then in the creation of the world, and finally in sending the Son and Spirit into the world, and the creation of the church. This is the meaning of revelation. To say that God is revelatory is to say that God's being opens itself to us by moving out of itself and coming to us in the world. This is why revelation should not be understood as communicating information. God is not a being who possesses information and then imparts it to humans. On the contrary, God's being is inherently and eternally revelatory because God is a Trinitarian life of outward movement that culminates in sending forth the Son and then the church in the power of the Spirit.

ELEVEN

New Testament Eschatology

Eschatology is customarily portrayed as either the doctrine about "last things" (judgment, resurrection, etc.) or the idea of the "last days" (the great tribulation, antichrist, the return of Jesus, etc.).

Without denying the importance of these meanings, I want to suggest that the New Testament shows a more important meaning. To understand this other meaning, we begin with the distinction, common in Jewish apocalyptic literature, between the present age and the age to come. The present age, in apocalyptic literature, is filled with evil. The age to come is characterized by (1) an outpouring of the Holy Spirit (Joel 2:28–29), (2) the new covenant (Jer. 31:29–31), (3) the transformation of the human heart (Ezek. 36:26–27), and (4) the appearance of the kingdom of God (Mark 1:15).

When Jesus appeared, he came preaching the arrival of the kingdom of God (Matt. 12:28). His ministry thus signaled the beginning of the age to come. In confrontation with the demons, in acts of healing, and in proclaiming good news to the poor, Jesus was actualizing the kingdom of God and introducing the age to come in the midst of the present age. At the Last Supper, Jesus established the new covenant—the fulfillment of Jeremiah 31:29–31 (Heb. 8:6–13). Following the resurrection, God poured out the Holy Spirit, an event that Acts 2 sees as the fulfillment of Joel 2:28–29. Finally, the promise of a new heart in Ezekiel corresponds to the New Testament's teaching about regeneration. So, with the appearance of Jesus Christ—his preaching, his works of power, his death, and his resurrection—the new age enters human history; the eschatological end of history has, in a sense, arrived: Satan has been bound, people are delivered from the evil powers of the present age, the dead are raised, and the good news of the kingdom is proclaimed.

The theology of the New Testament presupposes this realization of the eschatological end. It affirms that the end of the ages has come upon us (1 Cor. 10:11). It likewise proclaims that Christ appeared at the fulfillment of the present age (Heb. 9:26). It draws a clear distinction between the present, evil age (1 Cor. 2:6, 8; Gal. 1:4) and the age to come, which is not purely future but which, on the contrary, can already be tasted (Heb. 6:5). As 1 John puts it, "the darkness is passing and the true light is already shining" (2:8). In this context, the resurrection of Jesus has special meaning as a signal of the turn of the ages: the risen Christ was the firstfruits of the general resurrection (1 Cor. 15:20) and is the firstborn of the dead (Rev. 1:5). With his resurrection, the critical moment of the new age has occurred. In a sense, the former age has come to its end. Christ appeared when the fullness of time had arrived (Gal. 4:4).

Surprisingly, although the present, evil age had reached its end, it has continued to exist in tension with the new, messianic age of God's kingdom. Apocalyptic literature taught that the age to come would *replace* the present, evil age. What has happened instead is that the age to come continues to exist alongside the present, evil age. Unexpectedly, the present age did not end; it is still a reality. Because the age to come is also a present reality, there is a spiritual struggle between the two ages—a struggle that we experience in the conflict between flesh and Spirit (Gal. 5:16–17). There are, accordingly, two coexisting worlds: one of sin, the other of grace; one of flesh, the other of Spirit; the present darkness (Eph. 6:12) and the kingdom of God. Like a thief, Jesus has bound the strong man—Satan (Mark 3:27)—and has begun the task of overturning Satan's power by liberating people from demonic forces, disease, injustice, error, and oppression. At the same time, the present age of evil continues in power, and we feel its effects. The New Testament presents us with the conviction that the apocalyptic age to come was inaugurated in the ministry of Jesus. Since then, we have been living in the age to come while struggling with the residual reality of the present age.

So, while Christians confidently hope for an ultimate triumph of the age to come over the present, evil age (eschatology in the sense of "last things" and "last days"), we are already experiencing the age to come. Christian existence is thus an eschatological existence. It is an experience of the future, now in the present. That is why Colossians affirms we have already been raised up with Christ (Col. 3:1) and Hebrews asserts we have tasted the powers of the age to come (Heb. 6:5). Now, in the midst of history, we are living in the age to come, the age of the Spirit, the kingdom of God, and the new covenant.

Eschatology in Trinitarian Perspective

How does this understanding of eschatology relate to the Trinity? The connection lies in the fact that the age to come appears in history along with the sending of the Son and the Spirit. In other words, the age to come is another way of describing the Trinitarian appearance of God in history. The eschatological goal of history is the appearance of God in the time and space of human existence. That is why the book of Revelation portrays the end of history as God coming to dwell with humankind (21:3). This is also why the doctrine of the incarnation is the center of Christian doctrine. The idea of the incarnation is a way of affirming that God's will is to unite with humankind and that this is the purpose of human history. In Jesus Christ, God is united to human nature in a single person. In the Holy Spirit, God is united with a community, as a sanctifying and transforming power. All the hopes expressed in apocalyptic writings—the new covenant, the new heart, the kingdom of God, etc.—are simply various ways of expressing the belief that, in the age to come, God would unite with humankind, for this union brings about the new creation and sanctification.

The doctrine of the Trinity is an eschatological doctrine that explains why the age to come is an age of salvation. At the same time, we correctly understand eschatology only when we understand it in Trinitarian terms.

The Destiny of Creation

Let us now turn to eschatology understood in terms of "last things" and "last days." Although our tendency is to dwell on the lurid and sensational details of the book of Revelation, it is important to note that Paul's letters are interested in other matters. Consider, for example, these texts:

- "Then the end will come, when he hands over the kingdom to God the Father after he has destroyed all dominion, authority and power. For he must reign until he has put all his enemies under his feet. The last enemy to be destroyed is death. When he

has done this, then the Son himself will be made subject to him who put everything under him, so that God may be all in all" (1 Cor. 15:24-26, 28).
- "to be put into effect when the times reach their fulfillment—to bring unity to all things in heaven and on earth under Christ" (Eph. 1:10).
- "and through him [Christ] to reconcile to himself all things, whether things on earth or things in heaven, by making peace through this blood, shed on the cross" (Col. 1:20).

These important texts tell us that the universe as a whole is in a state of alienation because sin has disrupted God's lordship. Even though all things have been created through Christ and for Christ and all things hold together in Christ (Col. 1:16-17), the human world exists in a state of futility and corruption (Rom. 8:20-21) because of sin. In Christ, God is reestablishing lordship. The reconciliation of humanity in the church is a critical part of this lordship. When Christ has subdued every enemy, the created world itself will be reconciled to God, for according to Paul, the created order will eventually share in the "glorious liberty of the children of God" (Rom. 8:21, RSV).

Eschatology in the sense of "last things" thus has a Trinitarian basis. In the end, God the Father will be all in all because it is God the Father from whom all things come (1 Cor. 8:6). The created world comes from God the Father and finally is reconciled to God the Father. Just as the Son is the instrument by which God creates the world (John 1:1-4; Col. 1:16; Heb. 1:2), so the Son is also the instrument by which the Father reconciles the world and reestablishes lordship. That is why Paul said the Son reigns until all enemies have been subdued and then delivers the kingdom over to God the Father (1 Cor. 15:24-25, 28). Finally, the Son sends the Spirit into the world to accomplish recon-

> The church is the people who have been delivered from the authority of darkness and the present, evil age, and have been transferred to the kingdom of God.

ciliation in the church. So it is through the Spirit that the church offers the worship that constitutes reconciliation (since it is in worship that we recognize God's lordship and order our lives by it).

The Holy Spirit and Eschatological Existence

If it is true that the new age and the kingdom of God have appeared in the ministry of Jesus Christ, then history's eschatological end has arrived. Christian existence is thus an eschatological existence, an existence between the present, evil age and the final fulfillment of God's kingdom. As eschatological existence, the Christian life is, above all, life in the Spirit of God, for the Spirit is an eschatological reality; the gifts of the Spirit are the manifestation of the age to come.

To live in the Spirit is to experience the age to come and its power now. It is to experience the future world that God is creating in the midst of a present that can no more contain the new age than old wineskins can hold new wine. The Christian life is an eschatological existence that joins the old and the new. The Holy Spirit belongs to the future world that God is creating—a world in which all flesh receives the divine Spirit (Joel 2:28-29). In this future world, all flesh has the obedient heart and spirit that Ezekiel spoke of. In this future world God reigns, and God's kingdom prevails. To be a Christian disciple is to believe that this future world has begun to become a present reality and that the Holy Spirit is the manifestation of this reality in human life. To live in and by the Spirit, therefore, is to be delivered from the present, evil age and to escape the corruption of fleshly existence (Gal. 1:4; 5:16-17). It is, in short, to become holy—to become members of the people of God who live in utter devotion to God's kingdom.

The church, accordingly, is the eschatological community. The church is the people who have been delivered from the authority of darkness and the present, evil age, and have been transferred to the kingdom of God (Col. 1:13). The church is the people who have tasted the heavenly gift, who share in the Holy Spirit, who have tasted the good word of God, and now experience the powers of the coming age (Heb. 6:4–5). The church is the community that lives, in the present moment, the future that God is creating. As the eschatological people of God, the church is a community of the Spirit—the eschatological gift (Acts 2:38). In the church the gifts of the Spirit operate, and in the church the sanctifying power of the future becomes effective.

The eschatological nature of the church tells us there is an essential link between the Spirit and the sacraments. Baptism is an initiation into the new age—the washing that accomplishes rebirth and renewal in the Holy Spirit (Titus 3:5). In baptism the Spirit incorporates us into the body of Christ (1 Cor. 12:13). The Lord's Supper is likewise an eschatological event; it is an anticipation of the banquet of the kingdom of God (Isa. 25:6). In the Lord's Supper, the church eats a meal that looks forward to the fulfillment of God's kingdom. But this meal is not only anticipation—it is also a participation in that kingdom and its presence in the world. When we eat the Lord's Supper, we actualize the kingdom here and now. That is why, in many liturgies, the Eucharist is preceded by a prayer, the *epiclesis*, in which we pray for the Spirit to come upon the bread and cup and make them become for us the body and blood of Jesus. The prayer of *epiclesis* is a prayer that the Spirit will sanctify the bread and cup so that, by eating and drinking, we share in the body and blood of Jesus Christ (1 Cor. 10:16).

The Holy Spirit and the Ambiguities of Eschatological Existence

The church is the eschatological community—the community of the future age. The Christian life is eschatological existence. To believe as a Christian is to affirm the reality and power of the future in the present. However, the Christian life—the life of the future—is lived in the midst of the present, evil age. The kingdom of God is present with power, but its presence has not yet vanquished the present age. Paradoxically, the future age of the Spirit has not yet replaced the present, evil age but coexists with it (Heb. 2:8–9). This coexistence makes eschatological existence ambiguous. We feel this ambiguity in the struggle with sin, doubt, and despair. Although we are sanctified, we are subject to temptation. Although we have the Spirit as a down payment on the future, we may fall into doubt and perplexity. Even though the church is the community of the Spirit, it is also a community that experiences brokenness in the midst of redemption (Eph. 6:11–13; Phil. 3:12–16).

Take, for instance, the signs and wonders of the Spirit. The Bible testifies that the manifestation of the Spirit often comes with works of extraordinary power. At the same time, the New Testament knows that signs and wonders are, at best, highly ambiguous indicators of the Spirit. Mark 13:22, for example, warned about false prophets and messiahs who will perform signs and wonders. Revelation likewise cautioned the seven churches of Asia about the false prophet who would perform signs and wonders on behalf of the beast (Rev. 13:13–14; 16:14). Paul even tells us that Satan can appear as an angel of light (2 Cor. 11:14). The fact, then, that someone works a miracle is not necessarily proof of the Holy Spirit's presence; signs and wonders are inherently ambiguous, calling for discernment, even when performed in the power of the Holy Spirit. As Paul stated in 1 Corinthians 13:2, "if I have a faith that can move mountains, but do not have love, I am nothing." It is accordingly possible to work a miracle while failing to love. In such cases, the spiritual value of the miracle is zero.

Or, take the Spirit's guidance. As noted previously, the New Testament teaches that the Spirit leads the church into the truth and guides our conduct. But we experience this guidance ambiguously. There are thus two dangers: one is not listening to the Spirit at all; the other is conflating the Spirit's guidance with human feelings. The first danger is obvious, but the second occurs if we take hunches, beliefs, and assumptions to be the Spirit's guidance, when in fact they may simply result from the working of the human mind.

Additionally, the Spirit's guidance is not always as clear as we might wish. We have already noted Acts 21, where Paul learned through prophetic oracle that if he went to Jerusalem there would be trouble. The Christian disciples in Tyre, anxious about Paul, told him through the Spirit not to go (v. 4). Because they said this *through the Spirit*, we can say confidently they were not motivated simply by human affection for Paul. Their warning *was* inspired by the Holy Spirit. But Paul insisted on going to Jerusalem anyway, and the disciples finally decided it was God's will for him to do so (v. 14). Both Paul and his friends were led by the Spirit, but they reached contrary conclusions.

Similarly, Paul and Barnabas, both filled with the Spirit, disagreed mightily over the value of John Mark for their ministry. As a result, they went their separate ways (Acts 15:36–40). Likewise, Paul strongly urged Apollos to visit the church at Corinth; however, Apollos was not willing to do so at that time and indicated he would come when he had time (1 Cor. 16:12).

Here are cases where Spirit-filled Christians disagreed on important matters. Being filled with the Spirit does not guarantee either wisdom or right behavior. The church should constantly seek the guidance of the Holy Spirit, but such seeking will not eliminate disagreement, even among Christian disciples who are filled with the Spirit.

Spirit baptism seems wonderfully unambiguous—until we look more closely at the narratives in Acts. Besides the initial outpouring of the Spirit in chapter 2, Acts relates that the Samaritans had been baptized but could not receive the Spirit until the apostles laid hands on them (8:14–17). It states as well that the Holy Spirit fell onto Cornelius before he was baptized (Acts 10:44–47). What, then, is the relation between baptism and receiving the Spirit? And what is the relation between receiving the Spirit and the laying on of hands? Moreover, Spirit baptism is not a once-for-all event; Acts 4:31 records a fresh reception of the Spirit. So, on the controversial question of Spirit baptism and its relation to water baptism, it is best not to be too dogmatic. Sometimes the Spirit comes before baptism and sometimes after baptism.

Prophecy is likewise inherently ambiguous. The New Testament, while encouraging the prophetic word, issues many words of caution:

- While some are given the gift of prophecy, others are given the equally important gift of discerning spirits (1 Cor. 12:10).
- We should let prophets speak, but the rest of the congregation must sit in judgment over the prophets' words (1 Cor. 14:29).
- While not despising prophecies, we are to test everything, holding fast to the good (1 Thess. 5:20–21).

- We are not to believe every spirit but must instead test the spirits to see whether they are from God, for there are many false prophets (1 John 4:1).

These texts tell us that early Christians were aware of the ambiguous nature of prophetic speech. Even when it is uttered by sincere, Spirit-filled Christians, it may not express God's will and truth. As with miracles and with the Spirit's guidance, prophecy demands discernment by the church community.

Even sanctification shares in the ambiguities of eschatological existence because sanctification works at two levels. In one sense, to be sanctified is to be incorporated into the holy people of God by the divine acts of forgiveness, justification, and adoption. Paul affirmed that the Corinthians were sanctified in this sense (1 Cor. 1:2; 6:11). In another sense, sanctification is about attaining a Christlike character. The Corinthians fell short in this respect. Although they undoubtedly possessed the Spirit of God, their practice of the Christian life was far from ideal. To use the words of Galatians, they were alive in the Spirit but were not keeping in step with the Spirit (5:25). They were sanctified in the first sense of the word, but they were still people of the flesh (1 Cor. 3:1–3). And even when we have become holy in the second sense, we are still far from absolute, flawless perfection, if we take "perfection" to mean that we will never make mistakes again. Sanctification does not instantly make us wise, discerning people who possess flawless judgment and behavior. On the contrary, even the most holy people remain all too human in many respects. Sanctification thus shares in the ambiguities of eschatological existence.

The Historical Development of the Doctrine of the Trinity

Part II

TWELVE

Trinitarian Theology before the Council of Nicea

The doctrine of the Trinity was the first Christian doctrine to receive serious, church-wide attention and the first to receive formal statement in an ecumenical creed. Christian affirmations of the Trinity reflect the language of the ancient creed formalized by church councils. In this and the following four chapters we will follow the contours of the developments that resulted in the formation of the doctrine we affirm today.

Developments in Christology

The Legacy of the New Testament

Early Christian writings that formed the New Testament gave to Christian communities several enduring affirmations about Jesus Christ. However, attempts to understand the implications of these affirmations and to discover their coherence with other beliefs resulted in controversies in the second and third centuries.

The New Testament portrays Jesus as a human being in various texts. He is described as:

- A male human being (Acts 2:22).

- Being tempted (Matt. 4:1–10; Luke 4:1–13).
- Growing tired and thirsty (John 4:6–7; 19:28).
- Descended from David (Rom. 1:3).
- Born from a woman (Gal. 4:4).
- Having typical human emotions such as grief (Matt. 26:37; Mark 14:33–34; Luke 22:44), anger (Matt. 21:12–13; Mark 3:5; 11:15–17; John 2:14–17), and hunger (Mark 11:12).
- Growing in wisdom (Luke 2:52).
- Suffering and dying (the passion narratives in Matthew, Mark, Luke, and John).

The letter to the Hebrews adds a distinctive note to this portrait of Jesus's humanity: Jesus was made perfect through his sufferings (2:10), was like us in all respects except sin (2:14–18; 4:15), reverently submitted to God, and learned obedience through his sufferings (5:7, 8).

At the same time, several New Testament passages also present Jesus Christ as divine. There are a few unambiguous references to Christ as God; there are others that only imply Christ's divinity.

Unambiguous texts are found in John's Gospel:
- John 20:28, where Thomas calls Jesus "my Lord and my God!"
- John 1:1, which asserts that the divine Word is God.

More ambiguous passages include:
- Philippians 2:6, which asserts that, before his appearance in the world, Christ existed in the form (*morphē*) of God.
- John 10:30, where Jesus claims, "I and the Father are one."

There are a couple of passages (Titus 2:13 and 2 Peter 1:1) that *may* identify Christ as God, but the grammar is ambiguous. Likewise, there are some manuscripts of John's

Gospel that identify Christ as God in 1:18, but other manuscripts at this point refer to him as Son. Nonetheless, the New Testament documents bear witness to a growing early Christian belief in Christ's divinity. John 9 tells the story of the blind man who, at the end, bows down before Jesus (9:38). John 5:23 says we must honor the Son as we honor the Father. Revelation 5 shows the heavenly beings worshiping Christ just as, in chapter 4, they worshiped God the Father (5:8–14). We can safely say that first-century Christianity was moving steadily toward the practice of worshiping Jesus Christ, a practice that clearly implies belief in Christ's divinity.

How did first-century Christian writers think about the process by which the divine being became incarnate in the human being? Here the New Testament writers used a variety of terms.

- John's Gospel says the divine Word became flesh (1:14).
- In Philippians Paul speaks of the Son emptying himself, taking the form of a slave, being born in human likeness (2:7).
- Similarly, Romans asserts that God sent the Son in the likeness of sinful flesh (8:3).
- Hebrews affirms that the Son shared in all things human (2:14).
- 1 John repeatedly emphasizes that Jesus Christ came in the flesh (e.g., 4:2).

Second- and Third-Century Debates about Christology

The second and third centuries saw a proliferation of Christian writings. Among these writings are many that testify to a vigorous debate about how best to understand

Jesus Christ. These debates were governed by at least two assumptions that virtually everyone shared.

First, all early Christian writers, whether they were eventually deemed orthodox or heretical, believed that God's nature was incapable of suffering. This is the concept sometimes referred to as "divine impassibility." Such a belief generated considerable discussion about the nature of Jesus, who clearly had suffered pain and death. If Jesus suffered and died, and if God cannot change, how can Jesus be God? Did only his body die? Was his death real?

Second, all early Christians were committed to a form of monotheism. In the second century, monotheism was the belief that there is one supreme, eternal, and unchanging God. Such belief did not exclude belief in a multitude of lesser spiritual beings, which the pagans worshiped as gods. The Christian view was that, while these beings might be gods (lowercase g), they were not *God*—they were not eternal and unchanging. The need to preserve the unity of God (sometimes referred to as the "monarchy of God") meant that Christians could not simply regard the Son as a second God alongside God the Father. As a result, some subtle thinking had to occur in order to affirm the divinity of Christ without compromising the demands of monotheism.

One of the most pressing debates about Jesus Christ concerned his body. It seemed paradoxical to some that God would acquire a body, for being bodily subjects one to changes of all types, including suffering and death, something that poorly accorded with common belief about God.

How, then, were Christians to think about Christ's body? One stream of thought regarded Christ's body as a guise or appearance. The incarnation, in other words, was comparable to the way in which, in Greco-Roman mythology, gods were said to have appeared in human form. This belief avoided the problem of having God suffer and die, for in this case God did not *really* become human but instead only *appeared* human. The view that Christ only *seemed* to have a body and thus did not *really* suffer and die is often referred to as "docetism," from the Greek word *dokeo*, which means "to appear" or "to seem." The historical figure with whom we can most certainly identify docetism is Marcion, who lived in the first half of the second century. However, mainstream Christian thought insisted that Christ *had* truly suffered and died and, therefore, had a real body. One of the earliest postapostolic witnesses to this belief was Ignatius, bishop of Antioch (d. around 107), who emphatically taught that Jesus had suffered. Ignatius argued against any who believed that Christ's suffering had been a matter of mere appearance.

Another early Christian controversy centered on the physical body of Christ. Valentinus and his followers taught that Christ had a real physical body but that it was not a physical body like humans have; his body was instead composed of a heavenly material—it was a spiritual body. Valentinus also maintained a separation between the divine, spiritual nature of Christ and his physical body. The latter could suffer and die but not the former. So in the crucifixion Christ's body died, but his spiritual being did not die. This theory raised a critical question about the nature of the resurrection: had Jesus been—and will we be—resurrected in the flesh? What was the nature of Christ's resurrected body? Valentinus's school acknowledged that Christ was raised with a physical body but insisted that it was transformed into something spiritual. In response, Tertullian and other Christian writers asserted vigorously that Christ's body was a properly and fully human body and that the resurrection body is ordinary flesh. While acknowledging that the flesh will be transformed in the resurrection, they asserted that the resurrected, transformed body will nonetheless be the body in which we live today.

Mainstream Christianity thus came to affirm the suffering, death, and resurrection of Jesus Christ in a real and full sense. Christ's body was held to be really and truly human; his suffering and death were real. Consequently, Christians could also look forward to a resurrection of the flesh; the entirety of human nature, body as well as soul, participates in redemption.

These affirmations, however, did not settle all questions. Remaining unresolved were questions about the relation of the divine to the human in Christ, and the extent to which the divine in Christ suffered and died. Did admitting that Christ had suffered as a human, in the body, mean that Christ's divine nature also suffered? Did it die? These questions were taken up again in the fourth and fifth centuries.

Finally, let us consider one other controversy from early Christian history: when did Jesus become divine? This question, like the question about Christ's body, was closely related to the conviction that the divine nature cannot suffer or change in any way. If, then, Jesus suffered and died, did his suffering and death involve his divine nature?

One early way of thinking about this problem was to assert that divinity had descended upon Jesus at the baptism and then departed before the crucifixion. To support this view, the Gospel accounts of the descent of the Holy Spirit upon Jesus at his baptism were taken to mean that, prior to that time he had been a human being no different from the rest of us. In the baptism, the divine nature (the Christ) came upon him, and he became a man bearing this divine nature. In this way he was able to perform miracles and have miraculous knowledge. However, to whatever extent Jesus suffered, such suffering occurred *only* in his human nature; the divine nature remained unaffected.

And, since divine nature cannot die, the crucifixion was the death only of the human *man* Jesus; the divine nature—the Christ—had left him. This view is often called "adoptionistic Christology" because in it Jesus is regarded as a human being who receives divine status by virtue of his reception of the Christ at his baptism. It may more accurately be referred to as "possession Christology" because Jesus is a human being who temporarily possesses divinity. This view is associated with a few early Christians—Paul of Samosata, Cerinthus, and Theodotus—about whom little is known.

Against varieties of possession Christology, mainstream Christian writers asserted that Jesus Christ was divine from the beginning of his earthly life. This is one reason the affirmation of Christ's virginal conception was important; it showed that there was no time in his life when Jesus was merely human. On the contrary, he had been joined with divinity from conception. Additionally, the early mainstream writers argued for a closer connection between the divine and the human than the various possession Christologies allowed. They began to insist that, instead of Jesus merely receiving the divine nature, there had been a union of divinity and humanity. God had become fully incarnate in Jesus of Nazareth.

Logos Christologies

The form of early Christian Christology that proved to be the most influential for later centuries was the sort that used the idea of the divine *logos* as its leading conception.

Logos is a Greek word with many meanings, including "reason" and "word." The term was much used in Greek philosophical discourse before the Christian era. It appears in the first chapter of John's Gospel: "In the beginning was the Word, and the Word was with God, and the Word was God" (1:1). Although the idea of *logos* plays no further role in John's Gospel, Christian writers in the second century found it to be a useful notion for articulating some important christological convictions. Among these was belief in the Son's eternity and in the Son's distinction from the Father.

The idea of the divine *logos* gave Christian writers a way to think about the Son's eternity. If the Son is the Father's *logos*, then the Son must be eternal, for the Father, they argued, can never be without *logos*. To say otherwise would be to claim that God the Father could exist without rationality (another meaning of *logos*), or to claim that the Father somehow acquired *logos* at some time. Neither of these conclusions was acceptable to early Christian thought. The Son, then, as God's *logos*, was eternal—in the beginning with God the Father.

The idea of the *logos* also provided a way to distinguish the Father from the Son. This is one of the central issues of the doctrine of the Trinity: if the Son is God, is the Son a second God alongside the Father? This is impossible, for in that case we would believe in two Gods and thus destroy the unity—the monarchy—of God. Or, is "Son" simply a different name for God, so that the Son and the Father are one and the same being? This solution preserves the unity of God but destroys the distinction of the Son from the Father. By thinking of Jesus Christ as the incarnation of the *logos*, early Christians could preserve the unity of the Father and Son as well as their distinction. The unity lies in the fact that the Son is the *logos* of the Father—the Father's inmost word and expression. The distinction rests in the common difference that we draw between a speaker and the speaker's words. Although the words express the speaker's mind and thus have unity with the speaker, there is a meaningful distinction between the two; the words are not simply a name *for* the speaker but are a distinct reality.

The idea of *logos* yielded another dividend, giving early Christians a way to think about the origin of the Son. Built into the metaphor of sonship is the notion that the Son somehow *derives from* the Father. This notion is not clearly articulated in the New Testament, but early Christian writers pondered the Son's relationship to the Father, assuming some relationship of origin. The metaphor of *logos* provided a concept for conceiving this relation, for a word derives from the speaker's mind. The word is, so to speak, an extension of the speaker's mind. In this way, early Christians could think of the Son as (1) eternal with the Father, (2) distinct from the Father without being a second God, and (3) having his origin in the Father.

The Christology of Origen

The great theologian Origen (c. 184-c. 254) deserves his own section because of his important contribution to later discourse about Christology and the Trinity. There are three main points to his Christology: his view of the Son's eternal generation, the distinctions between the Trinitarian Persons, and the idea of subordination.

We have already seen that the idea of the *logos* gave early Christians a way to think about the Son's origin; however, it remained an open question whether the Son's origin from the Father was an act of creation. If it *was* an act of creation, then the Son is something created and belongs in the realm of the created world. In this case, it is difficult to see how the Son would deserve to be called God. But if the Son's origin is not an act of creation, what is it?

Origen's contribution to this issue lay in his assertion that the Son's origin from the Father (his being begotten) was not an act that took place in time; on the contrary, the Son is eternal, without beginning and without end. Accordingly the act whereby the Son comes to be from the Father is an eternal act, completely outside of time. With this view, Christian theology could meaningfully affirm that the Son derives his being from the Father without having to think of the Son as something created. Instead, according to Origen, the origin of the Son is unique, without analogy in the created world.

Origen also emphasized that the Trinitarian Persons are distinct—they are not simply different names for one being. Here Origen employed a term—*hupostasis*—that came to be much used in later Trinitarian discourse. *Hupostasis* is a Greek term with several meanings; it generally means "something real." Origen used it to assert that the Son and Spirit are distinct from the Father. God, in other words, is a Trinity of *hupostaseis*. Of course, Origen was not asserting the existence of three Gods; his use of *hupostasis* was an attempt to assert the distinction of the Persons of the Trinity—not their separation.

Finally, Origen's theology asserts a clear subordination of the Son and Spirit to the Father. There is, in other words, a ranking within the Trinity: the Father is first, the Son second, and the Holy Spirit third. The reason is that the Son and the Spirit derive their being from the Father; the Father alone is, to use the ancient terminology, "unoriginate," which means that only the Father does not derive being from another. With this idea of subordination, Origen was trying to do justice to biblical texts such as John 14:28, where Jesus says, "The Father is greater than I." In certain works, Origen seemed to represent the Son and Holy Spirit occupying a lesser stratum of divinity than the Father. In this view, the Father is God in the truest sense of the word. The Son and Spirit are divine by their derivation from the Father. This idea of subordination created quite a bit of confusion for Trinitarian theology in the future.

Developments in the Doctrine of the Trinity

Apart from Origen's contributions to Trinitarian thought, the most significant contribution came from Tertullian, who was born in the second century and died early in the third century. Tertullian's Trinitarian writings were directed against an idea that today we call "modalism," or "modalistic monarchianism." Modalism was attributed to people such as Praxeas and Sabellius, people about whom we know almost nothing, except the little bit reported by writers like Tertullian.

Modalism was an attempt to safeguard the unity (the monarchy) of God. To that end, modalists (of whom Tertullian named Praxeas as a proponent) strenuously asserted the unity of the Father, Son, and Holy Spirit. Tertullian interpreted Praxeas to mean there was no real distinction between the Trinitarian Persons. They were, in a word, merely differing names for, or *modes*, of the one divine person. The one divine being was in some respects Father, in other respects Son, and in other respects Holy Spirit. Praxeas, according to Tertullian, accused mainstream Christians of believing in three Gods because they affirmed that each person is a distinct *hupostasis*.

To combat modalistic thinking, Tertullian asserted that there is within God's life a dispensation (*dispensatio*), a Latin term he used to translate the Greek term *oikonomia*, a word that originally referred to the management of a household or other business. There is, Tertullian affirmed, within God a *dispensatio* or *oikonomia* (economy)—a sort of internal order that constitutes the Trinitarian Persons in their distinctness. In order to denote the Trinitarian distinctions, Tertullian borrowed the term *persona*, which originally referred to masks worn by actors. *Persona* (in English, "person") thus has the same use as *hupostasis* in the thought of Origen and other Greek writers. According to the divine dispensation (*dispensatio*), there are three *persona* within God. They do not differ in being or essence (*substantia*)— only in form.

Tertullian agreed that there is only one God, but this unity does not imply that God is a unitary being, without distinction. On the contrary, the unity is distributed into a Trinity through the dispensation within God's life. Tertullian also coined the term *trinitas* to denote the three persons. Tertullian's thoughts contributed much to the development of Trinitarian doctrine, especially in the Latin-speaking parts of early Christianity. All of the above terms became indispensable parts of the standard vocabulary of Trinitarian theology.

Meanwhile, Origen was making his own contributions to Trinitarian terminology. He used the Greek term *trias* to denote the Trinity; he used the term *homoousios* to describe the common essence of the Persons; and he coined the compound word "God-human" (*theanthropos*) to denote the incarnate Word.

Thanks to the combined efforts of Tertullian and Origen, by the mid-second century, the church had a valuable set of terms to describe the unity of God and the distinction of Persons, as well as the divine essence.

THIRTEEN

The Council of Nicea

By the year 300, the Christian church had seen two centuries of vigorous debate and discussion about Jesus Christ and the Trinity. There was comparatively little debate about the Holy Spirit, mostly because christological and Trinitarian matters occupied most of the available energy for debate. Nonetheless, by around 300 there was broad agreement in the church on some fundamental points.

In particular, the church's leaders firmly rejected every version of docetic Christology; they just as emphatically affirmed that Christ's body was a fully human body. Moreover, they repudiated possession Christologies (adoptionism) and energetically rejected any suggestion that Jesus became divine at his baptism or that he only temporarily received the divine nature. In Trinitarian matters, the church had turned away from modalistic understandings of the Trinity, insisting that Father, Son, and Spirit are *hupostaseis*—distinct but not separate or divided. At the same time, the church confessed the full unity of God and never allowed belief in the three *hupostaseis* to overrule its commitment to monotheism.

This broad consensus was challenged in the fourth century when the church faced its longest and most divisive debate about the Trinity. New and difficult christological questions arose. The period from 325 to 451 thus saw the appearance of the first four ecumenical councils and several resulting creeds.

The Theology of Arius

The debate about the Trinity began in the early 300s when a priest named Arius in Alexandria, Egypt, began teaching that the Son had a beginning. With this assertion, Arius exposed an issue that had not previously been settled, although it had been discussed. At the heart of the matter was the question *what does it mean to say that the Son was begotten?*

The language of begetting comes from John's Gospel. In four passages (1:14, 18; 3:16, 18) it refers to Jesus Christ as the *monogenes* Son. Scholars today are likely to translate this term with words such as "unique" or "only." However, in the early centuries of Christianity, theologians generally took it to refer to the act of procreation—hence the use of the archaic English word "beget" in the King James Version. Taking the metaphor of Father and Son literally, or at least seriously, they believed John's Gospel was asserting that the Son owes his being to the Father. Early theologians thus took affirmations about the Son's being *monogenes* to be descriptions of the act by which the Father generates (to use a neutral term) the Son. The Son, in other words, has his origin in the Father. This idea of origin explains why early Christian writers were attracted to the idea of God's *logos* (see the discussion on *logos* Christologies in chapter 12).

The question that had never been settled—but which Arius undertook to settle—was whether the Son's coming forth from the Father meant the Son had a beginning in time. Was the Father ever alone, without the Son? Or, instead, was the Son eternal, without beginning? What is the meaning of *monogenes*, and what does it imply? For Arius, it was obvious that if the Son is generated, then the Son must have a beginning, just as earthly sons have a beginning when they are generated by their parents.

The New Testament did not provide easy answers to these questions. According to John's Gospel, the Word was in the beginning with God, but it leaves unanswered what that beginning was. The beginning of the world? Of time? Of the Son? Colossians 1:15 says the Son is the firstborn of all creation. What does that phrase mean? Arius took it to mean the Son was the first of God's creations—that the Son was not eternal but instead had a beginning in time.

Moreover, there were lingering questions from Origen's theology. On one hand, Origen had affirmed that the Son is eternal; on the other hand, he taught that only the Father is without origin, the Son having an origin in the Father. The leftover question was, does the Son's having an origin establish an essential difference between the Father and the Son? Is the Father alone God in the proper sense because only the Father is without origin? Does the Son occupy a diminished rank of divinity because he has an origin?

There were other residual issues. As in the second century, the issue of Christ's suffering entered the conversation. All parties in the debate agreed that God cannot suffer or change in any way. How, then, can Christ be God if he suffered and died? Additionally, there was the question of whether the Father generated the Son by an act of will or by virtue of the Father's nature. If it was an act of will, then the Son would seem to be something created, like everything else. If it was by God's nature, then (according to the logic of the times) God would be subject to natural necessity, compromising God's freedom. Finally, the church had never fully come to terms with the idea of subordination. John 14:28 affirms that the Father is greater than the Son. What did this mean? Origen believed that it implied a ranking among the Trinitarian Persons, the Son occupying the second rank and the Spirit the third. What were the implications of this subordination?

Arius began to teach that the Son has a beginning and that the Son was the first of the Father's creations. He thus interpreted *monogenes* rather literally as "born," and held that birth implies a beginning. In this way, Arius denied that the Son is God, because, in order to be God, the Son would have to be eternal—without beginning. By affirming that the Son has a beginning, Arius was denying the divinity of the Son. This bundle of convictions came to be encapsulated in the phrasing, "there was (a time) when the Son was not."

The Council of Nicea

Arius's views proved both popular and controversial. He was evidently a quite popular teacher in Alexandria, and his teaching spread throughout the churches of Egypt, Palestine, and Syria. At the same time, the bishop of Alexandria, named Alexander, took issue with Arius's teaching and sought to correct his theology. Arius resisted this correction, and controversy ensued. Before it was over, churches in virtually every part of the Roman Empire were drawn into the debate, which raged throughout the entire fourth century and, in some places, beyond.

The controversy became so divisive that the Roman emperor, Constantine, who was desperate to maintain peace after years of civil war, convened a meeting (a council) of bishops for the purpose of resolving the dispute about Arius's theology. This council met in Nicea, in modern-day Turkey, in 325. Around three hundred bishops comprised the council. They represented, for the most part, the Greek-speaking portions of the church; there were few, if any, bishops from Latin-speaking churches. Nonetheless, this was by far the largest council to have met, so it came to be regarded as ecumenical—that is, representative of the entire church.

The council quickly rejected Arius's theology; however, it had a more difficult time finding Trinitarian language the bishops could agree on. Eventually, the council fashioned an acceptable creed; however, some of the language was open to more than one interpretation, which required a second council later in the century (Constantinople, 381) to clarify.

The Creed of Nicea

Here is a literal translation of the creed the council produced:

> We believe in one God, Father, world ruler, Maker of everything visible and invisible. We believe in one Lord, Jesus Christ, the son of God, generated [or, begotten] from the Father *monogenes*, that is, from the being [*ousia*] of the Father, God from true God, generated, not made, of the same being [*homoousios*] as the Father, through whom all things have come to be, both in heaven and on earth, who for us humans and our salvation came down and became flesh and was incarnated, suffered, and rose on the third day, and ascended into the heavens, and is coming to judge the living and the dead. And in the Holy Spirit. The catholic church curses those who say that there was [a time] when he was not, and that he was not before he was generated, and that he came to be from nothing, or who say that the Son of God is from some other *hupostaseis* or being [than that of the Father], or is capable of turning or change.

Let us examine the creed, phrase by phrase.

We believe in one God. Here the church reaffirmed its commitment to the monarchy of God and to monotheism. Nothing that is affirmed in the doctrine of the Trinity should be construed in such a way as to compromise this commitment.

Father. In keeping with the New Testament, the creed immediately identifies God as the Father.

World ruler. This is a traditional affirmation unrelated to the Arian controversy.

Maker of everything visible and invisible. This phrase is a residual response to Marcion's theology. Marcion argued that God, the Father of Jesus, was not the Creator; the world was instead created by a lesser being. The creed here affirms that God the Father is the Creator.

We believe in one Lord, Jesus Christ. This is drawn from Ephesians 4:4–6: "There is one body and one Spirit, just as you were called to one hope when you were called; one Lord, one faith, one baptism; one God and Father of all, who is over all and through all and in all."

The Son of God. This affirmation reflects consistent New Testament language about Christ. It was not part of the Arian controversy.

Generated from the Father (*monogenes*). This phrase is a summary of affirmations in John's Gospel.

From the being (*ousia*) of the Father. To this point, the creed has said nothing that relates to the Arian controversy; Arius could agree with everything said so far. However, by stating that the Son was generated from the being of the Father, the creed dissents from Arian theology, which asserted that the Son was created from nothing, as were other creatures. *Ousia* is a Greek work with several meanings. When the creed was translated into Latin, *ousia* was translated as *substantia*, "substance." Depending on context, *ousia* can mean "being" or "essence." In philosophical discourse, it refers to that which is real. Unfortunately, *hupostasis* also denotes that which is real. The two terms *ousia* and *hupostasis* at the time had nearly identical meanings. This fact caused considerable confusion and debate in subsequent decades.

God from true God. This phrase elaborates on the preceding phrase. The Son is God, proceeding from or generated by the Father, who is true God.

Generated, not made. This is a direct and express rejection of Arius's theology, according to which the Son was created. The creed here asserts that, while the Son has an origin in the Father, "origin" does not mean "creation." The Son is eternal, without beginning. Being made or created would imply that the Son had a beginning.

Of the same being as the Father. In Greek, this phrase is simpler: *homoousios* with the Father. *Homoousios* means having the same *ousia* that the Father has. This is a different way of affirming the full divinity of the Son. The Son is God in every sense of the word. Having an origin in the Father does not in any way compromise the Son's divinity.

The next several phrases relate to human salvation and were not controversial in the Arian debate.

And in the Holy Spirit. The lack of controversy surrounding the Holy Spirit is indicated by the shocking brevity of the affirmation. The creed says virtually nothing about the Spirit; it would be left to later councils to make a fuller affirmation.

The creed ends with curses directed toward those who assert fundamental Arian theses, using an indirect reference to Galatians 1:9: "As we have already said, so now I say again: If anybody is preaching to you a gospel other than what you accepted, let them be under God's curse!" The purpose of the creed and of these closing curses is to publicly and definitively establish orthodoxy as opposed to heresy.

The Aftermath of the Council of Nicea

The council and its creed did not immediately put the Arian controversy to rest. There remained a small number of bishops who were convinced adherents of Arius's theology; an even larger portion of bishops, probably a majority, rejected Arius's theology but found serious problems with the creed. Eusebius of Caesarea, author of *Ecclesiastical History*, was a leading member of this group. They had concerns about using philosophical terms, particularly *homoousios* and its meaning of "same *ousia*." They interpreted *ousia* as denoting an *individual being*. So, for them, the Father is one *ousia*, and the Son is a second *ousia*. In other words, for them *ousia* and *hupostasis* ("person") were identical in meaning. Accordingly, they saw in the creed's affirmation of *homoousios* the claim that Father and Son are the same being, the same individual divine Person. This was the error of modalism.

Further, the creed's assertion that the Son is from the *ousia* of the Father seemed to be saying that the Son is taken from a part of the Father, as though the Father's being had been divided into portions. These bishops argued that the Son is a distinct being (*ousia*) from the Father; however, they also claimed that the Son is *like* the Father in every way (*homoiousios*). These two terms (*homoousios* and *homoiousios*) can be confusing since they spell alike except for the second letter "i" in the latter. Nonetheless, they convey significantly different theological ideas pertaining to the Trinity.

Defense of the creed fell mainly to Athanasius (d. 373), bishop of Alexandria after Alexander. In a voluminous series of writings, he set forth his understanding of the creed and of *homoousios* and defended it against objections. The key for Athanasius was to understand *ousia* not as denoting an *individual being* but instead as denoting a common *nature* or *essence*. To say that the Son is *homoousios* with the Father is to say they share a common divine essence, not that they are one and the same being. For Athanasius, each is a *hupostasis* of the one divine *ousia*; the one, indivisible divine *ousia* exists concretely in three *hupostaseis*.

Athanasius did not have an easy job convincing other bishops; his task was complicated by the fact that the fortunes of the Arian and the Nicene parties depended in part on which emperor was ruling—some emperors supporting the Arian party, others supporting the Nicene party. Nonetheless, as the century wore on, support for the creed gained momentum. This process culminated in the second ecumenical council, which met in 381 in Constantinople. It fully affirmed the Nicene Creed and then issued its own expanded creed, which spelled out some of the implications of Nicea and clarified its teaching.

FOURTEEN

Post-Nicene Developments in Christology

The creed of Nicea, though it established once and for all that Christ was fully divine, did not fully resolve other lingering issues about the Trinity. One particular issue—the relation of Christ's human nature to his divine nature—was not addressed by the creed. This issue set off a divisive debate in the middle of the fourth century. In particular, the debate focused on the key question "In what sense is Jesus Christ human?" John's Gospel affirmed that the divine Word became flesh, but what exactly did that entail? The Gospels report that Jesus thirsted and became tired, that he suffered and died. How do these human characteristics relate to Christ's divine nature? The debate over this issue, which raged over a century, is complicated since it involved several leading Christian thinkers and their controversial perspectives. In this chapter we will briefly summarize these perspectives and conclude with the view that was finally adopted by the Council of Chalcedon in 451.

The debate in its early stages centered on two differing views: one view affirmed that when the divine Word (*logos*) became flesh (incarnation), divine nature so thoroughly united with and mixed with human flesh that Jesus was a single, divine person, and that Christ lacked a human mind. When Jesus spoke and acted, it was God in the flesh who spoke and acted, not a human being with divine power. By virtue of having a living human body, the incarnate Word could be hungry, tired, and suffer, but Jesus Christ is a single, divine subject; all thought and action arises from the divine *logos*. In other words, whatever Jesus said and did was a function of his divinity; none of his words or actions were of a human being. The key proponent of this view was Apollinarius of Laodicea; his Christology is sometimes referred to as a Word-Flesh Christology.

The other view, promoted by Diodore of Tarsus, saw a clear distinction between Christ's human nature and his divine nature. Thus, anything in Christ's earthly life related to suffering or limitation was a function of his human nature; anything supernatural was a function of his divine nature. In other words, Jesus Christ is really two subjects, one human and the other divine. For Diodore, it was important that Jesus's sufferings and limitations pertain strictly to his humanity, that his divinity not be compromised. Whereas Apollinarius spoke of a mixing of divine nature and human flesh in incarnation, Diodore spoke of the divine Word indwelling the human Jesus.

In the latter half of the fourth century, Gregory of Nazianzus (d. 389) introduced another view into this debate, which on the one hand agreed with Apollinarius's view of the unity of Jesus Christ but on the other hand disagreed with him on the nature of Christ's humanity. Gregory proposed that the incarnation of the *logos* involved the union of divine nature with a full and complete human nature. Jesus, in other words, had a human mind as well as a human body. Gregory argued that in order for God to redeem human nature, it was necessary for the *logos* to be united with the totality of that nature; any element of human nature not united with divinity would be left out of redemption. At the same time, with Apollinarius, Gregory affirmed that Christ's identity is fundamentally his divinity. Jesus Christ is God, who is united with human nature; he is not a human being who bears divinity. Consequently, worship of Jesus Christ is not worship of a human being; it is worship of God, who is united to human nature.

The debate on the subject of Christ's human nature continued in the fourth and fifth centuries; different centers of Christian theological thinking—Rome, Alexandria, Antioch, and Constantinople—were drawn into the debate. Rome and Antioch were most concerned to emphasize the full and complete humanity of Christ and to avoid attributing suffering to Christ's divine nature. Alexandria was most concerned to maintain the utter unity of Christ and to regard Christ as fundamentally divine. As a result, Rome and especially Antioch were comfortable thinking of Jesus being two subjects of experience, while Alexandria generally thought of Christ having one single nature.

The christological debate accelerated when Nestorius (d. 451) became bishop of Constantinople. Nestorius discovered that the liturgy in Constantinople referred to Mary as *theotokos*—"the one who bore God." Nestorius took this to mean that Mary had given birth to God, a conclusion that shocked him. It seemed to him as though the church was confessing that Mary was somehow the mother of God. Nestorius, like Diodore of Tarsus, drew a distinction between the human nature of Christ and his divine nature. He was willing to grant that Mary was the mother of Christ (*christotokos*)—that is, of Jesus Christ's human nature—but he could not tolerate the suggestion that Mary was the mother of the *logos*. (Theodore of Mopsuestia, Nestorius's predecessor and a follower of Diodore, also emphasized the full humanity of Christ, which for him meant that Christ was not simply God. In some circumstances, Jesus acted as God; in other circumstances, he acted as a human.)

As with Diodore and Theodore, Nestorius was concerned about any implications that God's nature could suffer or change; he was a staunch upholder of God's immutability (the idea that God cannot change) and impassibility (the idea that God cannot suffer). Nestorius's efforts to change the liturgy led to a major controversy, reigniting the issues surrounding the previous debate between Apollinarius and Diodore. In particular, Nestorius engaged in a violent debate with Cyril (d. 444), patriarch of Alexandria, who—in the tradition of Apollinarius and Gregory of Nazianus—affirmed the absolute unity of Christ and his fundamental identity as God. To advance his view, Cyril introduced a term: the union of natures in Christ was a union according to the *hupostasis*, and was, therefore, a "hypostatic union." What Cyril meant by this term was that the incarnation resulted in a single *hupostasis*—a single subject. Jesus (for Cyril) was the *logos* enfleshed, a single being and subject, a union of the *logos* and human nature. To Nestorius and his supporters, talk of such union implied a mixing or blending and thus a confusion of natures, so that Jesus was neither divine nor human but a mixture.

In some ways, the debate between Cyril and Nestorius (and his supporters, as many others joined the debate) hinged on the question of Jesus's suffering. As we have seen, Nestorius represented a tradition for which any talk of the *logos* suffering was anathema; Cyril, however, with his strong view of Christ's unity, was comfortable with the notion that the *logos* suffered and died in Christ's flesh. Cyril was careful to acknowledge that the *logos* did not suffer in its divine nature, it being impossible for God to suffer.

Nonetheless, the union with human nature made the *logos* capable of suffering and dying in the flesh with which it was hypostatically united.

The Council of Chalcedon

The christological controversy of the late fourth and fifth centuries became so contentious that councils were convened to resolve the conflict. Some were regional councils, but two were ecumenical: Ephesus in 431 and, more important, Chalcedon in 451. The Council of Chalcedon produced a creed that has had lasting importance in the history of Christianity. It is a compromise document; both sides—Cyril and the supporters of Nestorius—had to concede certain points and soften their claims in order for a consensus to emerge.

Here is a literal translation of the creed:

Following the holy fathers, we all, in agreement, teach [people] to confess one and the same Son, our Lord Jesus Christ, the same perfect in divinity, the same perfect in humanity, the same truly God and truly human, possessing a rational soul and a body, *homoousios* to the Father according to divinity and *homoousios* to us according to humanity, in all respects like us except for sins. Before the ages [he was] generated from the Father according to divinity, in these last days he was generated from Mary, the virgin, the *theotokos*, according to humanity, for us and our salvation, one and the same Christ, the Son, Lord, *monogenes*, recognized as possessing two natures, unmixed and unchanging, without division and separation, the distinction of the natures being in no way nullified because of the union, but instead the distinctive properties of each nature being preserved, and running together [or coinciding or concurring] in one person and one *hupostasis*, not divided or cut into two persons, but one and the same, *monogenes* Son, God the *logos*, the Lord Jesus Christ. Just as the prophets [taught] about him and the Lord Jesus Christ himself taught us and as the creed of the fathers has handed down to us.

Let us examine the creed more carefully, focusing on the points of controversy.

Following the holy fathers. This is the creed's way of asserting that its teaching is continuous and consistent with prior statements of faith, especially the creeds produced by the ecumenical councils.

One and the same Son, our Lord Jesus Christ. This statement underlines the unity of Jesus Christ. Jesus is a single subject of action and experience, not two subjects.

Perfect in divinity, the same perfect in humanity, the same truly God and truly human, possessing a rational soul and a body, *homoousios* to the Father according to divinity and *homoousios* to us according to humanity, in all respects like us except for sins. This affirmation says that Jesus Christ is the union of a full and complete divine nature and a full and complete human nature, which implies a rejection of Apollinarius's view and affirms that Jesus had a human mind.

Before the ages [he was] generated from the Father according to divinity, in these last days he was generated from Mary, the virgin, the *theotokos*, according to humanity. This phrase affirms Mary's status as *theotokos* but clarifies that Jesus was generated from Mary only according to his humanity—the eternal *logos* was not generated from Mary. This preserves Cyril's affirmation of *theotokos* but concedes the Nestorian position that Mary was involved only with the generation of Jesus's humanity.

Possessing two natures, unmixed and unchanging, without division and separation, the distinction of the natures being in no way nullified because of the union,

but instead the distinctive properties of each nature being preserved, and running together [or coinciding or concurring] in one person and one *hupostasis*, not divided or cut into two persons, but one and the same, *monogenes* Son. This statement clarifies that Jesus Christ is the union of two distinct natures. It further states that the union was not the result of some mixing or merging of the two natures, a point that the Nestorian party insisted on. It also affirms that the union is a real unification—the two natures cannot be separated from each other. At the same time, the union of the natures does not diminish the divinity of the divine nature or the humanity of the human nature. The union leaves both natures intact, with all of their essential properties. Finally, the union results in a single *hupostasis*, a single person (in Greek, *prosopon*). This reflects Cyril's concept of the hypostatic union. There are not two sons, the human son and the divine Son. There is instead a single, indivisible person, one Son, who is fully divine and fully human.

The creed of Chalcedon was intended to be a definitive statement of the church's faith regarding Jesus Christ, but it was also intended to bring differing parties together. It was partially—but only partially—successful. Many churches in the eastern part of the empire, as well as all the churches in the western part of the empire, accepted the creed. However, there continued to be Christians who espoused Nestorius's Christology. They were initially concentrated in Syria, but because of threats from the Roman Empire, they moved eastward into Iran, Iraq, India, even reaching as far as China. These Christians continue to exist today.

Additionally, there was a significant group of churches that were deeply suspicious of the Chalcedonian creed's affirmation of Christ's two natures. Its talk about their union did not assuage their suspicion that the creed had compromised the unity of Jesus, that it affirmed the existence of a distinct, human Jesus alongside the divine *logos*. These churches refused to accept the creed of Chalcedon, which explains why today some Eastern churches identify themselves as Orthodox and others do not; in this context, "orthodox" denotes those churches that accept Chalcedon. The dissenting churches, located in the eastern parts of the Christian world and in Egypt, were thus regarded as non-orthodox. They came to be called monophysite churches, since (according to the Orthodox churches) they argued for Christ having a single (*monos*) nature (*physis*). These churches exist today; however, they reject the name monophysite, affirming Christ's two natures while insisting strenuously on his absolute unity. There has been, in recent years, dialogue between representatives of Orthodox and non-Chalcedonian churches with a view toward eventual reestablishment of communion and mutual recognition.

Postscript to the Creed of Chalcedon

As noted, debate about Christology did not end with the Council of Chalcedon. Within a couple of centuries the debate shifted to the question of whether Christ had a human will besides the divine will of the *logos*. The Council of Chalcedon affirmed that Christ had a rational soul (i.e., a human mind), thus rejecting the view of Apollinarius. But the question arose of whether Christ's human mind included a will. The question hinged on an obvious issue: if Christ had a human will besides the divine will, could the two wills conflict? The alternative view, that Christ had two wills, followed from the logic of Chalcedon: if Christ possessed a full and complete human nature, he must have a human will, but there must be a complete unity of wills. The matter was settled at the third council of Constantinople (680–681), which decreed that Christ had two wills in perfect union.

Post-Nicene Developments in the Trinity and Pneumatology

The focus of theological discourse in the period 325 through 451 was Christology. The Council of Nicea settled the question of Christ's divinity; the Council of Chalcedon established the relation of the divinity to Christ's humanity. Nonetheless, a secondary debate occurred regarding the Holy Spirit (pneumatology is the study/understanding of the Holy Spirit).

The Debate about the Holy Spirit

This pneumatological debate was similar to the dispute about Arius's theology in that it involved the full divinity of the Spirit. It was provoked by a group known as Macedonians; there is much about this group we do not know because their writings, if they had any, no longer exist. Their main claim was that the Holy Spirit is not a divine person, or *hupostasis*, as the Son is. They accepted the faith of the Nicene Creed that the Son is fully divine, but they seem to have regarded the Spirit as a power from God but not as a Trinitarian Person. They especially objected to worship being directed toward the Spirit.

The main respondents to the Macedonians were the brothers Basil of Caesarea and Gregory of Nyssa. In their refutation of the Macedonians, they made several arguments to establish the full divinity of the Holy Spirit.

First, they argued for the Spirit's divinity on the basis of the Spirit's acts. The Spirit, they asserted, is the agent of immortality, life, and sanctification. They understood salvation as a divine work actualized in human lives by the Spirit. The fact that these actions are attributed to the Father and to the Son, as well as to the Spirit, establishes that the Spirit is coordinated with the Father and Son and dwells in the same rank of divinity. They also claimed that we have access to God the Father through the Son, but we have access to the Son only in the power of the Spirit.

Second, they pointed out that in the Bible the sorts of attributes ascribed to the Father and to the Son are also ascribed to the Holy Spirit. The Spirit is said to be holy, righteous, and good, just as are the Father and Son. Since the Holy Spirit shares in divine attributes and performs divine acts, the Spirit, they concluded, must be God. Likewise, the Spirit is present everywhere in creation; such omnipresence is a divine attribute. Additionally, lying to the Spirit is a sin (Acts 5:1–11). Since one can sin only against God, such lying argues for the Spirit's divinity. So, the Spirit's having divine attributes adds to our sense that the Spirit is coordinated with the Father and Son in divinity.

Third, they argued that there are no gradations of divinity. The Spirit, in other words, is not a lesser God, or divine without being fully divine. There is, they stated, nothing between Creator and created—no intermediate being. All of creation lies on one side of an ontological chasm; God stands on the other side. The Holy Spirit is, accordingly, either fully divine or not divine at all. The fact that the Spirit is named in the third place (as in Matthew 28:19, which lists the Father, Son, and Holy Spirit) establishes no sort of hierarchy or subordination among the Trinitarian Persons, who are equal in power and glory. Instead, this ordering corresponds to the pattern of divine activity whereby all things begin with the Father, proceed through the Son, and are completed in the Spirit.

Fourth, they argued that, just as the Father is never without the Word and Son, so the Son is never without the Spirit. The Spirit is the Spirit of the Son. Just as it is inconceivable that God the Father could lack *logos*, so it is inconceivable that the Son could lack the Spirit.

The First Council of Constantinople

The dispute with the Macedonians plus the need to resolve the debate surrounding Apollinarius's theology resulted in a second ecumenical council, which met in Constantinople in 381. The council produced a creed that built on the Creed of Nicea but augmented it in important ways. This second creed, in fact, ended up replacing the Creed of Nicea. Today, when we recite the Nicene Creed we are actually reciting the creed that resulted from the council at Constantinople.

Here is a literal translation of the creed:

We believe in one God, Father, world ruler, Maker of heaven and earth, of all things visible and invisible. And in one Lord, Jesus Christ, the Son of God, the *monogenes*, who was generated [or begotten] from the Father before all the ages, light from light, true God from true God, generated, not made, *homoousios* with the Father, through whom everything has come to be, who for the sake of us humans and our salvation came down from heaven and became flesh and human from the Holy Spirit and from Mary the virgin, being crucified for us under Pontius Pilate and suffering and being buried and rising on the third day according to the scriptures, and ascending into heaven and sitting at the right hand of the Father, and coming again with glory to judge the living and the dead, whose kingdom will have no end. And in the Holy Spirit, the Lord and Maker of life, who proceeds from the Father and with the Father and Son is worshiped and glorified, who spoke through the prophets. [And] in one holy, catholic, and apostolic church. We confess one baptism for the forgiveness of sins. We look forward to the resurrection of the dead and the eternal life to come. Amen.

This creed repeats much of the original Nicene Creed; however, there are important additions.

It adds that the Son was generated from the Father before all the ages, to guard against anyone thinking that the Son was generated as an act of creation in time. In other words, the creed here affirms Origen's belief in the Son's eternal generation.

To the original creed's affirmation that the Son is God generated from true God—that is, from the Father, it adds that the Son *is* true God, ensuring that the Son is not regarded as occupying a lesser degree of divinity.

Most important, it adds considerably to the original creed's statement about the Holy Spirit. It declares the Spirit to be (1) the Lord and (2) the Maker of life. Like Gregory of Nyssa and Basil of Caesarea, it affirms the Spirit's divinity on the basis of the Spirit's divine attributes (Lord) and activity (Maker of life). It asserts as well that the Spirit is to be worshiped and glorified as the Father and Son are to be worshiped and glorified. It includes a note about the Spirit's traditional role in prophetic inspiration. Finally, it asserts (in an allusion to John 15:26) that the Spirit proceeds from the Father. As we will see, this later became a controversial matter.

The creed of Constantinople thus strengthened the church's affirmation of the Son's full divinity and stated for the first time the Spirit's divinity. Although it did not use the term *homoousios* of the Spirit, it clearly asserts that the Spirit is God and thus marked an advance on the original creed of Nicea. It thus became the definitive doctrinal statement of the Trinity.

A Postscript: The *Filioque* Controversy

After the Council of Constantinople, the Christian church experienced one more Trinitarian controversy of great magnitude. It had to do with the text of the creed from Constantinople.

As noted above, the creed states that the Holy Spirit proceeds from the Father. By this affirmation the creed means that, in eternity, the Spirit is breathed forth by God the Father just as the eternal Word is spoken by God the Father. "Proceeding" or "procession" thus describes the eternal relationship of the Holy Spirit to the Father, just as "generating" or "begetting" describes the relationship of the Father to the Son.

Several centuries after the Council of Constantinople, a version of the creed began to be used in Latin-speaking parts of the church. In this Latin version, the creed stated that the Spirit proceeds from the Father *and* from the Son. This version asserted that the Spirit proceeds not from the Father alone, as the original version seems to imply, but from the joint action of the Father and the Son. The phrase "and from the Son" is in Latin a single word, *filioque*. As a result, the ensuing debate has been called the *filioque* controversy. It is also sometimes referred to as a debate about

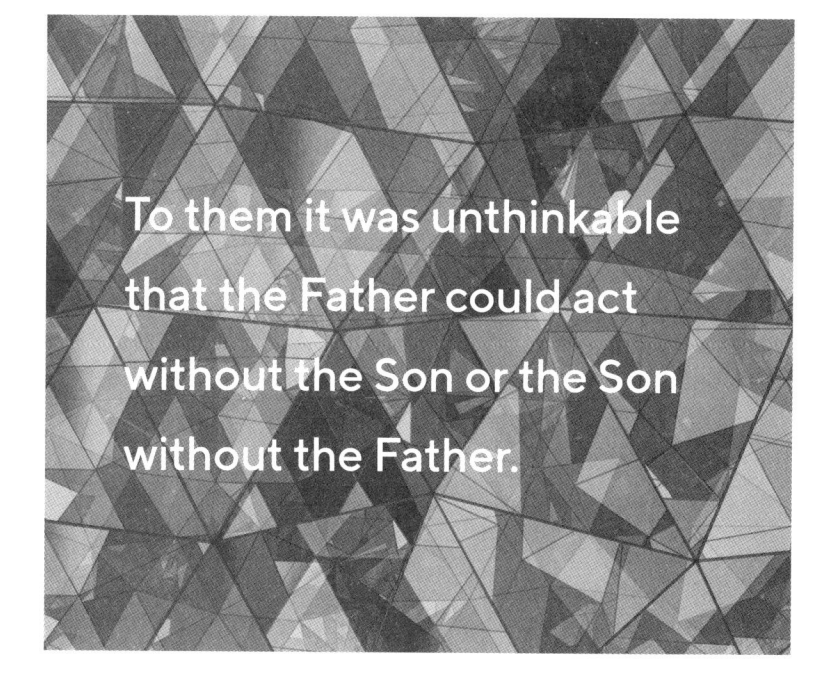

> To them it was unthinkable that the Father could act without the Son or the Son without the Father.

the double procession of the Spirit, since in the Latin view the Spirit proceeds from the Father and the Son.

The controversy began when churches in the Greek-speaking part of the world noticed the different version used in Latin churches. The disagreement rested on two points. First, the Greek-speaking churches felt that no church had the right to change the creed. The creed, it was felt, depicts the truth about God and therefore should not be changed. Second, the Greek-speaking churches rejected the *filioque* phrase because they believed it is unsupported in Scripture. John 15:26 speaks of the Spirit proceeding from the Father, but they could find nothing in the Bible about the Spirit proceeding from the Father *and* from the Son. Consequently, they strongly objected to the version of the creed used in Latin-speaking churches.

On their side, it seemed obvious to the Latin churches that the intent of Constantinople was not to exclude the Son from the Spirit's procession, since the entire Trinity participates in every divine act. To them it was unthinkable that the Father could act without the Son or the Son without the Father. They also called attention to New Testament texts that described the Holy Spirit as the Spirit of Jesus, thus establishing a clear biblical link between the two. Additionally, the western churches insisted that the Spirit's procession must be different from the Son's generation, for otherwise why is the Spirit not a second Son? If both proceed independently from the Father, it becomes difficult to distinguish the procession of the Spirit from the generation of the Son. Finally, talk of the Spirit proceeding from the Father *through* the Son had been traditional in the west at least since Tertullian.

The controversy dragged on for centuries, becoming quite acrimonious and contributing to formal estrangement between the eastern and western churches in 1054. The longer the controversy endured, the more adamant each side became about the rightness of its own position.

During the Middle Ages discussion took place between representatives of the eastern and western churches in an attempt to heal the breach. The Second Council of Lyons (1245) crafted a compromise formula whereby churches would confess that the Spirit proceeded from the Father *through* the Son. Unfortunately, this compromise was ultimately rejected by the leaders of the churches. Since then there has been no official change. However, the animosity between East and West has been significantly reduced; the issue has simply shrunk in importance. Today, relations between the churches are ruled more by a spirit of charity and compromise.

SIXTEEN

Wesleyan Trinitarian Theology

156 Wesleyan statements of Trinitarian faith fall within the tradition of the ecumenical creeds. The following exposition will use these abbreviations to indicate which statement of faith is being referenced:
- UM: United Methodist Church's Articles of Religion
- AME: African Methodist Episcopal Church's Articles of Religion
- FM: Free Methodist Church's Articles of Religion
- W: Wesleyan Church's Articles of Religion
- N: Church of the Nazarene's Articles of Faith

Wesleyan statements about the Trinity begin where the ecumenical creeds begin, with an affirmation of God's unity, speaking variously of the unity of the Godhead—that is, of the divine nature (UM, AME, FM)—or of belief in one God (W, N). They also assert that the Trinitarian Persons are one: in substance, power, and eternity (UM, AME); in eternity, deity, purpose, power, wisdom, and goodness (FM); in essential nature, power, and eternity (W); and in essential being (N).

Wesleyan statements also make express reference to the Father, Son, and Spirit, using, except for the Nazarene Articles of Faith, the traditional term "person." The Nazarene statement says that God is "revealed as Father, Son, and Holy Spirit" and that Jesus Christ "was eternally one with the Father."

In describing the Persons, the Wesleyan Church alone has an article on the Person of the Father. It describes the Father as the source of all things and, with the Son and Spirit, as Creator of humankind in the divine image.

The longest Trinitarian section in these statements of faith pertains to Christology. Using a variety of language, they all affirm that Jesus Christ is God. Christ is very and eternal God (UM, AME); God in the flesh (FM); truly God (FM, W); the only begotten Son of God (W); and the second Person of the triune Godhead (N). The United Methodist and AME statements also employ the creedal idea of *homoousios*, asserting that the Son shares one divine substance with the Father. The statements thus all share the ecumenical creeds' rejection of Arian theology.

These statements include affirmations of Christ's two natures, speaking of the union of two whole and perfect natures (UM, AME, N); of Christ joining together the deity of God and the humanity of humankind (FM); and of Christ being truly God and truly man (W). In this way they demonstrate agreement with the Creed of Chalcedon. They also introduce the virginal conception of Jesus in order to establish his humanity: the Son took man's nature in the womb of the blessed Virgin (UM, AME) and was born of the Virgin Mary (FM, W, N).

With respect to the unity of the incarnate Son, the statements affirm that the two natures were joined together in one person, never to be divided; whereof is one Christ

(UM, AME); were joined together (FM); and are united in one Person (N).

Finally, all of the Wesleyan statements include the ecumenical creeds' anti-docetic affirmation of Christ's suffering and dying.

Regarding the Holy Spirit, the Wesleyan statements affirm the full divinity of the Spirit: the Spirit is of one substance, majesty, and glory with the Father and the Son, very and eternal God (UM, AME); the third Person of the Trinity, one with the Father and Son, equal in deity, majesty, and power (FM); truly and eternally God (W); and the third Person of the triune Godhead (N). As with the statement on Christology, the United Methodist and AME statements also affirm that the Spirit is of one substance with the Father and Son. Finally, all of these statements, except for the Nazarene article, affirm the *filioque*, asserting that the Spirit proceeds from the Father and the Son.

Thinking about the Trinity Today

Part III

SEVENTEEN

Continuing Trinitarian Controversies

The creation of creeds and the meeting of councils have not brought controversy about the Trinity to an end; on the contrary, there continue to be a number of movements at the periphery of mainstream Christianity whose theologies are non-Trinitarian.

Unitarianism

One result of the Protestant Reformation was the proliferation of new religious movements, along with renewed energy for studying Scripture in a fresh way. Although the commitment to Scripture was mostly beneficial for the life of the church, the freedom to study the Bible allowed for the reappearance of interpretations that mainstream Christianity had long since dismissed. One such interpretation resulted in the movement eventually known as Unitarianism.

The origins of Unitarianism lie in the theology of Faustus Socinus (1539–1604). His study led him to reconsider Arian theology. His theology proved to be influential, especially in Poland, where his movement grew to appreciable numbers. One of the principal documents of his movement in Poland is the Racovian Catechism, which sets forth the basis of modern Unitarian theology:

- God is a unitary being, not a Trinity of eternal Persons.
- Jesus Christ was human, not divine.
- Jesus is called the Son of God because God caused his miraculous, virginal conception.
- The Holy Spirit is not a Trinitarian Person but is instead a name for God's power in its operation.

Socinian theology migrated to England, where from the 1690s it found an audience among Protestants. By around 1800 Unitarianism was fully established as a religious movement, increasingly moving away from traditional Christian beliefs of all sorts. In 1961 the American Unitarian Church merged with the Universalist Church of America; today it calls itself the Unitarian Universalist Association. Additionally, the movement known as Christadelphia espouses a Christology that is essentially that of the Racovian Catechism. It also denies the Trinity of Persons and regards Jesus Christ as a human being.

The Church of Jesus Christ of Latter-day Saints

The Church of Jesus Christ of Latter-day Saints (LDS) has a distinct and, from a Christian perspective, highly unusual view of the Trinity. It is, in effect, a variety of polytheism. LDS teaches that God the Father has many children; Jesus was the first, but the rest of us humans are also children of the Father. Consequently, Jesus is not, in the words of the ecumenical creeds, the only begotten Son of God. He is merely the first and greatest. Additionally, the Father and Son are not *hupostaseis* of the one, indivisible, divine being. Instead, they are regarded as distinct beings ("personages"). Curiously, the Son is not the only divine Person to be incarnated; the Father also is said to possess a body of human flesh.[1] LDS theology thus has no place for the traditional affirmation that there is one God who exists in three *hupostaseis* or persons. On the contrary, it believes in many divine beings, of whom Father and Son are two. The Holy Spirit likewise is not a divine *hupostasis*. Instead, the Spirit is yet another distinct being. The only unity in God that LDS theology acknowledges is a unity of love and will among the three "personages;" there is no unity of *ousia* (being).

The Watch Tower Bible and Tract Society of Pennsylvania

The theology of the Watch Tower Bible and Tract Society of Pennsylvania, better known as the Jehovah's Witnesses, is Arian. Unitarianism had distant roots in Arian theology but finally came to the view that Jesus is human, whereas Arianism regarded Jesus as a superhuman spiritual being. Watch Tower theology agrees with Arius; for them, Jesus Christ is the angel Michael. He is thus not divine and not eternal; he is a creature, a being whom God created before the creation of the world. The Holy Spirit is likewise not a Trinitarian Person but is instead a name for God's power as it is exercised in certain ways in the world.

Oneness Pentecostal Theology

In the early part of the twentieth century, a debate occurred within the American Pentecostal movement. The churches in the movement were officially Trinitarian; how-

---

1. *The Doctrine and Covenants of the Church of Jesus Christ of Latter-day Saints: Containing Revelations Given to Joseph Smith, the Prophet, with Some Additions by His Successors in the Presidency of the Church*, Doctrines and Covenants 130:22, https://www.churchofjesuschrist.org/study/scriptures/dc-testament/dc/130.22?lang=eng#21.

ever, a few preachers began proclaiming that baptism ought to be performed in the name of Jesus only, instead of the traditional formula (in the name of the Father, and of the Son, and of the Holy Spirit). They based this view on Acts 2:38, where Peter commands the crowd to be baptized in the name of Jesus Christ.

From this change in liturgy there evolved a reconsideration of God's nature. Within a short time, some began teaching that God is not a Trinity of *hupostaseis*, or Persons. Instead, they held, God is a single Person. The proper name of that person is Jesus Christ. The terms Father, Son, and Holy Spirit refer not to *hupostaseis* of the divine being but to ways that God is revealed; the terms refer to divine functions. When the Bible wishes to describe God as transcendent, it refers to God as Father; when it describes God as incarnate in the world, it refers to God as Son; when it describes God as indwelling humans, it refers to God as Holy Spirit. But it is one and the same divine Person who is being described with these three names. This view came to be called Oneness Pentecostalism.

Oneness Pentecostal theology is a modern version of ancient modalism, according to which Father, Son, and Spirit are simply names of the one divine Person. It differs from ancient modalism in its severely Christocentric focus—the eternal God's name is Jesus Christ. Otherwise, it bears remarkable similarity to modalistic theologies of the second and third centuries.

Controversies about the Holy Spirit

The most pressing theological issues today are ecclesiological—the question about the nature and mission of the church. As a result, debate about Trinitarian issues has shifted from concerns prevalent in the first four centuries of Christianity to the intersection between the doctrine of the

Trinity and ecclesiology. As a result, Trinitarian controversy today is focused on the doctrine of the Holy Spirit.

Apart from the aberrant pneumatological teachings of groups such as the Latter-day Saints and the Watch Tower Society, debate today pertains to practical matters of church life and practice. The main one relates to the question of prophecy and other spiritual gifts. The question is, to what extent may the church today expect to experience the intensity of spiritual gifts that the book of Acts reports for the first-century church?

Some historical illustrations may help us see the point. Starting sometime in the second century there was a movement that we today call Montanism. Montanists were Christians who were alarmed that prophecy seemed to be dying out in the church and who sought to restore its importance; they accordingly emphasized the power of the Spirit. Among other controversial practices, they acknowledged that women could be prophets; they would not stand in the way of the Spirit if the Spirit gave the gift of prophecy to a woman. Montanism was not well received by mainstream Christianity, which was nervous about the Montanists' view of women and also their expectations that the end of the world was near. These beliefs, combined with their emphasis on Christian prophecy, put them out of step with the emerging mainstream of the Christian church. In fact, however, Montanists were attempting to recreate the life of the first-century church, at least as they understood it. The ancient controversy surrounding Montanism raises the question of the ministry of the Spirit in the church, especially with respect to what today seem like extraordinary gifts of the Spirit.

Another episode in Christian history that illustrates the problem comes from the early days of the Protestant Reformation in Germany. While German Reformers under the guidance of Martin Luther were instituting changes in worship, a group of men arrived proclaiming themselves to be prophets. They arrived (they believed) to help move the Reformation in the right direction. Among their beliefs were several that were far too radical for even the most radical Protestants:

- God reveals God's will directly to people in dreams and visions. Humans, therefore, don't really need the church or even the Bible.
- Because individuals communicate with God directly, we have no need of sacraments.
- God had revealed that the Turks would destroy Europe.

These self-proclaimed prophets also claimed miracle-working power and the ability to read the minds of others. Luther and most other German Reformers were not impressed with the prophets and dismissed their claims.

The illustrative movement that most readers will be familiar with is the modern Pentecostal movement. The beginning of the movement is usually dated to 1900 or 1901 when, at a Bible school in Topeka, Kansas, a student began speaking in tongues. In 1906, a revival occurred in Los Angeles, sparked by several people in a church meeting who began to speak in tongues. These foundational events launched a movement that today accounts for approximately 25 percent of all Christians. Although speaking in tongues is one of the more prominent practices of Pentecostalism, it is in fact part of a larger attempt to restore original Christianity as described in the New Testament, with the full range of spiritual gifts and offices.

These historical moments show that there has always been in Christianity an impulse to relive the spiritual power of the first-century church. Of course, it is important that we not exaggerate the intensity of early Christian spirituality. It is true that worship in Corinth was loud and dramatic; however, it would be a mistake to make the experience at Corinth normative. After all, this was the most problematic of all of Paul's churches. Its worship is not exactly the model that we should imitate.

Or, take the description of the church that we find in Acts. We certainly find signs and wonders, tongues and prophecy. But careful readers will note that the great majority of these take place in the opening chapters. When Acts gets around to describing worship in later chapters, we hear stories about Paul droning on so long that someone falls asleep (Acts 20:7–12). This episode indicates what a more normal worship service was like in the first century. It wasn't always signs and wonders; sometimes it was sleep-inducing sermons. Nonetheless, there has always been a segment of the Christian world that felt it important to recreate the signs-and-wonders atmosphere described in Acts and 1 Corinthians.

How should Wesleyans think about and relate to movements such as modern Pentecostalism? Wesleyans rightly have an ambivalent attitude. On one hand, some Wesleyans, especially those in the Holiness tradition, feel a deep affinity with such movements because the Holiness Movement understands itself to be a movement of the Spirit recapturing the power of early Christianity. That is why the Holiness Movement identified entire sanctification with the baptism in the Spirit. It interpreted Acts 2 to be the moment when the disciples were entirely sanctified. Like Pentecostalism, the Holiness Movement believed it was the result of God's final pouring out of the Spirit on all flesh. So there are points of deep similarity between Holiness Wesleyans and Pentecostal Christians. However, there are two main problems that Wesleyans find in modern Pentecostalism.

The first is the way some—not all—Pentecostal Christians insist, often loudly, that speaking in tongues is the one and only proof that someone has been baptized in the Holy Spirit. Although it is important to be sympathetic with Christians in other branches of the Christian tradition, and although it is just as important to be humble when we discuss doctrinal matters, this claim about tongues is unfounded. It has no basis in Christian experience and flatly contradicts the Bible. Paul stated plainly that no one possesses *all* the gifts of the Spirit (1 Cor. 12:4–30, especially 29–30). And, while he certainly allowed tongues in worship, it cannot be said that he eagerly advocated their practice (1 Cor. 14:1–19, 39).

Additionally, we should note that the "tongues" mentioned in Acts 2 are foreign languages, whereas the "tongues" mentioned in 1 Corinthians are unintelligible speech. Nowhere else in the New Testament is there a mention of the phenomenon of tongues as described in 1 Corinthians, which gives us the strong impression that speaking in tongues was not only problematic but may also have been limited to the church in Corinth.

Wesleyans, preferring to err on the side of grace, will not object to people speaking in tongues, even in the Corinthian manner—as long as the rules that Paul established in 1 Corinthians 14 are observed, but there is no biblical justification for insisting that speaking in tongues is the infallible sign of being baptized with the Spirit.

The second problem Wesleyans have with movements like modern Pentecostalism is the generation of extreme and unhealthy phenomena. There is much to like and admire in Pentecostal Christianity, but it often allows and perhaps even encourages odd behavior and beliefs. These include but are not limited to:

- Varieties of the health-and-wealth gospel of prosperity. This is the teaching that there is no good reason for Christians to be sick or financially stressed. Sufficient faith will bring untold prosperity and blessing.

- Word-of-faith theologies. These are cousins of the health-and-wealth message. The emphasis here falls on right speech. By avoiding talk of sickness and troubles and instead confessing faith in God's blessings, we can unlock spiritual forces that will benefit us.

- Extreme views of Christian prophecy. Especially in the last thirty years or so, a movement has arisen claiming to have prophetic powers. In the 1980s and 1990s, for instance, a group known as the Kansas City Prophets appeared. Today a quick search of the internet reveals a large number of sites devoted to relating predictions, warnings, and promises uttered by prophets. Some of these (such as exhortations for Christians to be faithful) are harmless, but others are peculiar and potentially dangerous (like prophets telling specific people that God wants them to do specific things).

- Visions, trips to heaven, and other unusual experiences. A common theme in the online world of prophecy is that the prophet had a vision or a trip to heaven in which God delivered a specific message to that prophet.

- The New Apostolic Reformation is a movement dedicated to restoring certain first-century ministries, especially the office of the apostle. The problem here is that the apostles answer to no higher human authority; they are responsible only to God. The Christian church long ago learned that such authority is a recipe for mischief and disaster.

Movements that claim to be of the Spirit but are not subject to some governing authority and have a low regard for the church's traditions inevitably produce eccentric sub-movements. These sub-movements typically move quickly in the direction of strange and harmful beliefs and practices.

As the Corinthian example shows, Spirit possession can be made to serve the flesh. The Corinthians undoubtedly possessed the Spirit. They lived in the Spirit, but they failed to walk in step with the Spirit. On the contrary, they sought to manipulate the Spirit's power and gifts to further their own ends. The challenge for Wesleyans, as for all Christians, is to ensure that the Spirit *leads us* and to avoid trying to *lead the Spirit* for our purposes.

Why are there such controversies surrounding the Holy Spirit? The reason is that the experience of the Holy Spirit is an eschatological phenomenon. It is the present experience of the age to come. A movement as epochal as the change from the present, evil age to the messianic age involves momentous tensions as one world passes away and the final hour before the new age arrives (1 John 2:17–18). The old cannot contain the new (Mark 2:21–22); disciples enter the emerging kingdom in acts of spiritual violence (Matt. 11:12); Satan, the strong man, is bound (Mark 3:27). Such tension cannot help but call forth extreme phenomena and behavior.

At the same time, Christianity is a religion of order and routine, ritual and liturgy. This reality is evident in 1 Corinthians 14, where Paul addresses Christian worship. Faced with numerous people in the congregation attempting to speak in tongues and prophesy simultaneously, Paul lays down the law: at most, two or three may speak in tongues, one at a time, and only if someone can interpret. Similarly, two or three may prophesy, one by one, with the congregation weighing what they say. Above all, everything must be done with dignity and order (1 Cor. 14:26–33, 40). For Paul, the extraordinary experiences of the Spirit must not result in disorder.

Christianity, then, balances contrary forces. On one hand there is freedom, spontaneity, and novelty of life in the Spirit; on the other hand there is need for structure and order. Order without freedom and spontaneity is deadly; freedom without structure becomes chaotic. Paul encouraged prophetic oracles but at the same time asserted his authority as an apostle to ensure order. Prophecy is to be welcomed, but the congregation must test the spirits to see if they are truly from God (2 Cor. 11:13-15; 1 John 4:1-6).

Finally, spiritual gifts and other things associated with the Holy Spirit attract controversy because of their eschatology. The question here is, to what extent can the kingdom of God be actualized in history? Christianity is based on the belief that with the life, death, and resurrection of Jesus a new, messianic age has arrived—the kingdom of God. This belief is woven into every Christian doctrine. But Christians have always disagreed on the extent to which God's kingdom has arrived. Granted that it has been inaugurated, is it still mostly in the future? How much of the kingdom's power and presence may we expect in the midst of history? Movements such as Pentecostalism have a highly realized eschatology, in which the blessings and power of God's kingdom are available now. Segments of the Pentecostal world would go further and say that the kingdom's blessing and power are *fully* available now. For them, there is no justification for Christians to be sick and poor and distressed. God's material blessings should prevail and *will* prevail if we simply exercise faith.

This view is represented in 1 Corinthians, where Paul said to the Corinthians, "Already you have all you want! Already you have become rich! You have begun to reign—and that without us!" (4:8). The Corinthians, possessing the Spirit, believed they were ready to receive the full range of blessings from the coming age. Over against this, Paul set his own suffering: "We are weak, but you are strong! You are honored, we are dishonored! To this very hour we go hungry and thirsty, we are in rags, we are brutally treated, we are homeless" (vv. 10–11). Paul was thus well aware that the eschatological blessings of the kingdom are available to us only in part. The rest requires the fulfillment of God's kingdom at the end of history.

There will always be some degree of tension between those for whom life in the Spirit opens up the full range of eschatological blessings and those who feel the kingdom and its blessings remain, for the most part, in the future.

EIGHTEEN

Some Continuing Perplexities about the Trinity

Within the parameters of orthodox Trinitarian belief, there are important issues on which a consensus has not been reached.

The Meaning of *Hupostasis* and *Persona*

There is no avoiding the fact that the doctrine of the Trinity is filled with technical terms. Few other doctrines have demanded as extensive a repertoire of terms in order to clarify main points and avoid misunderstanding. Yet students of the doctrine have understandably often found the technical terms not merely less than fully helpful but actual obstacles to understanding. The great theologian Augustine (354–430), struggling to come to grips with the doctrine and its terminology, asked in exasperation:

> Why, therefore, do we not call these three [Father, Son, and Spirit] together one person, as one essence and one God, but say three persons, while we do not say three Gods or three essences; unless it be because we wish some one word to serve for that meaning

whereby the Trinity is understood, that we might not be altogether silent, when asked, what three, while we confessed that they are three?[1]

Yet, when the question is asked, What three? human language labors altogether under great poverty of speech. The answer, however, is given, three persons, not that it might be [completely] spoken, but that it might not be left [wholly] unspoken.[2]

The theological community has developed the Trinitarian vocabulary not in order to probe into divine mysteries but so that the church can avoid utter silence in its proclamation. Christianity is a religion of the word; it must proclaim a message. If it is to escape silence altogether, it must use words; it must talk about God as revelation provides. The words are inadequate, but they are necessary.

Among the more challenging Trinitarian terms are *hupostasis* and its Latin equivalent, *persona*. As we noted in chapter 13, there was confusion about *hupostasis* even in the fourth century. Early in the century, *hupostasis* was interchangeable with *ousia* ("being, nature, essence"). This is why so many bishops objected to the Nicene term *homoousios*—it seemed to imply that the Father and the Son are the same being, without distinction. Later in the century, theologians began using *hupostasis* to denote that the Father, Son, and Spirit are three and *ousia* to indicate that the three Persons are one; hence the formula one *ousia*, three *hupostaseis*. *Hupostasis*, then, eventually came to denote each Trinitarian Person in distinction from the other Persons. In the

---

1. Augustine, *On the Trinity*, 7.6.11, http://www.newadvent.org/fathers/130107.htm.
2. Augustine, *On the Trinity*, 5.9.10, http://www.newadvent.org/fathers/130105.htm.

West, Tertullian used the Latin word *persona* to do this, and *persona* became the standard Latin term for this purpose.

However, using a term is one thing; clarifying a concept is another. What exactly is being said when we say that God is one *ousia* in three *hupostaseis*, or *persona*? The challenge for Trinitarian thought is to steer a course between two alternatives. On one hand, we might think of the Persons as merely names of the one God, or as ways in which the one God acts, or as appearances of the one God, or as modes of revelation of the one God. On the other hand, we might think of the Persons as separate beings, as individuals who are unified only in purpose and thought and not in being. Mainstream Christianity has decided against these alternatives. The former it labels modalism, charging that it can't make sense of the incarnation, in which the divine Word is clearly distinct from God the Father. The church likewise rejects the second alternative—which amounts to belief in three gods (polytheism) as an affront to its commitment to monotheism. The term *hupostasis* is an attempt to thread the needle by choosing a word with an ambiguous meaning and intentionally using it to denote the region of meaning between these two alternatives.

In our situation today, the one thing against which we must guard is transferring to *persona* all of the meaning borne by the contemporary words "person" or "personality." The Trinitarian Persons are not *personalities*—not three separate beings each with its own personality. Such a belief is another version of belief in three gods.

So what are the Persons? How are we to think of them? Are there, in the Trinity, three intellects and three wills? Or one intellect and will? The church's commitment to monotheism rules out the first option. In the Trinity we do not have three beings who share the same or similar thoughts and wishes. Instead, there is one single divine intellect and will. But does this not negate the distinction of the Persons? Are we not thereby back to some version of modalism? The answer is no—because the one divine intellect and will is the joint operation of the entire Trinity. Instead of thinking of the Father as doing certain things (e.g., creating) and the Son doing other things (e.g., redeeming) and the Spirit doing still other things (e.g., inspiring), we should think of creating, redeeming, sanctifying, and every other divine operation as a work of the entire Trinity in its absolute unity. Each work begins with God the Father, is mediated through God the Son, and is completed in God the Spirit. What is true of God's work in the world is true of God's eternal life. God's intellect, will, and in fact every aspect of the divine life is a movement from the Father, through the Son, perfected in the Spirit. There is thus no division of labor in the Trinity. Each person is fully at work in each Trinitarian action; none of the persons is an independent source of action.

Gendered Language

Augustine's puzzles about the language we use in discourse about God does not stop at the meaning of technical terms. In recent years, the theological community has become sensitive to its use of unnecessarily gendered language. We have learned, for example, to stop using "man" as a generic term and to employ instead other words, such as "humankind" or "humanity."

In recent years, the language we use in discourse about God has encountered another challenge; how do we speak about God without resorting to the gendered language in the Bible and in the Christian tradition that depicts God using masculine nouns and pronouns? There is consensus among Christian theologians today that the divine nature is not exclusively masculine. Christian theologians also recognize the fact that human language about God in the Bible and in the Christian tradition cannot be taken literally, since the transcendent God, the God who is infinite, cannot be contained in finite categories such as gender, which limit the ways something can exist. What this means is that none of the Trinitarian Persons is exclusively masculine. It may be valuable to think of God as having characteristics we typically think of as male *and* female. Or, it may be helpful to think of God as simply transcending gender altogether. At any rate, it is incorrect to think of God as possessing one gender exclusively.

This acknowledgment raises a problem for Trinitarian theology, as well as for translating the Bible and using it in worship. The language of Father and Son has the sanction of Scripture and of tradition. Theology cannot simply banish such language. Even if we did so, we would have to find alternative language. Yet the use of such language subtly conveys the idea that God really *is* masculine in an exclusive sense, which unfortunately reinforces the dangerous patriarchal tendency of the Christian tradition. What then are we to do?

Let us consider a specific instance: does the Holy Spirit have a gender? The confusion here arises for several reasons. For one thing, in ancient languages all nouns (such as "spirit") were assigned a grammatical gender, much as they have in modern languages like Spanish, French, and German. But the grammatical gender of "spirit" differs according to ancient language. The Hebrew word for spirit, *ruah*, is feminine; the Greek word, *pneuma*, is neuter; the Latin word, *spiritus*, is masculine. Curiously, John's Gospel, written in Greek, contradicts the grammatical rules by using both neuter and male pronouns for the Holy Spirit.

How, then, should we think of the Spirit with respect to gender? It seems obvious that the Spirit is not a *thing*, so we can rule out the neuter gender. That leaves masculine and feminine. Should we choose one over the other? Or alternate between them, sometimes using "he" and other times using "she"? Using both at different times would be awkward and potentially confusing. At the same time, using one gender exclusively is clearly unacceptable. God is neither male nor female, or at least is not one of them exclusively. It is true that the first Person of the Trinity is called Father and that the second Person is called Son. But these are symbols—metaphors. It would be a mistake of the highest order to infer that any of the Trinitarian Persons is male on the basis of a title or an image. It is vital to acknowledge that the Holy Spirit is not gendered.

We have essentially two options. One option is to continue to use the traditional language. In this case, pastors and teachers have a moral obligation to constantly remind the church and its members that these terms are metaphors and not to be taken literally. They do not imply anything about God's gender. The other option is to use more neutral language. Some have suggested that in place of Father and Son we use Parent and Child. Alternatively, we could use the New Testament's language of God, Word, and Spirit. However it is done, it is time for the church to move beyond our tradition of patriarchal, gender-exclusive language.

NINETEEN

Knowing the Trinity

The doctrine of the Trinity and other Christian doctrines seem simultaneously simple and complex—complex because of the subject matter but simple because, after all, it is merely words in sentences. The doctrines seem to consist of declarative sentences of the sort we use every day. However, students and practitioners of theology must attend carefully to the nature of theological discourse and words when dealing with divine matters. Words are never a simple matter, and sentences will have more than one function. What, then, is the meaning of Trinitarian affirmations? How is theological discourse functioning in the doctrine of the Trinity?

Doctrine as a Rule of Faith

One way in which Christian doctrines function is as rules of faith. In this capacity, a doctrine such as the Trinity distinguishes truth from error; it establishes the boundary between acceptable belief and unacceptable belief. It demarcates a space within which belief and understanding can happen, and a boundary outside of which there is danger. As a rule of faith, a doctrine is not a verbal description of God but is instead a prescription for thinking, believing, speaking, and acting.

The history of the doctrine of the Trinity can accordingly be interpreted as the exploration of scriptural texts and the implications of those texts. In this history, many interpretations were eventually found to be inadequate. Take, for instance, the various christological beliefs of the second and third centuries: adoptionistic Christologies, docetic Christologies, Arius's theology, and so on. One way of understanding the development of the doctrine of Christ, culminating in the creed of Chalcedon, is to see it as the attempt to maintain the paradox of the incarnate Word—the Word that is divine and human—and therefore as the rejection of every belief that softens the paradox. Thus, docetic Christologies must be rejected; they resolve the paradox of the incarnation by eliminating Christ's real humanity. Adoptionistic Christologies fail because they do not affirm the real union of the divine and the human; Arius's Christology is wrong because it fails to affirm Christ's divinity. The great debates in the fourth and fifth centuries surrounding Apollinarius and Nestorius and Cyril of Alexandria were all concerned with this question: shall we proclaim the paradox of the incarnation or instead resolve the paradox by making Christ something less than the perfect union of humanity and the divine *logos*? Accordingly, the church rejects Apollinarius's views because it compromises Christ's full humanity; Nestorius's theology falls short because it seems to lack a fully unified person of Christ. In each case, belief is measured by its ability to maintain the paradox of the God-human Word; beliefs that soften the paradox are rejected.

The same holds true for the doctrine of the Trinity. As a rule of faith, it is concerned not with giving us a mental image of the Trinity but only with guarding against any belief that would diminish either the Trinity of Persons or the unity of God.

The resulting doctrine of Christ is thus a statement *of* the paradox. How, then, is it functioning? Does it provide us with a concrete and sufficient picture of the incarnate Word? Does it give us a model by which to think about the Word? Does it yield an exhaustive understanding? No, it does not. It does not tell us what it means when it says that the divine suffered in the flesh without suffering in the divinity. It does not tell us what it meant experientially for Jesus to be tempted. Instead, the Chalcedonian doctrine of Christ, functioning as a rule of faith, tells us first of all what we should *not* believe. We should not think of Jesus Christ as less than fully God or as possessing divinity without a real union. We should not think of Christ as only apparently human or as somehow deficient in humanity. We should not think of Jesus Christ in any way that portrays him as other than the complete union of divinity and humanity.

The same holds true for the doctrine of the Trinity. As a rule of faith, it is concerned not with giving us a mental image of the Trinity but only with guarding against any belief that would diminish either the Trinity of Persons or the unity of God. Hence, modalistic views are unacceptable because they overemphasize the unity at the expense of the Trinity of Persons. Arius's theology likewise does not allow for a real Trinity of divine Persons. At the same time, the doctrine rules out any temptation to overemphasize the Trinity of Persons with a resulting belief in three divine beings. Does the doctrine of the Trinity, as expressed in the ecumenical creeds, tells us how we are to picture the three and the one? Does it give us a concrete model by which to understand the Trinity? No, it does not. As a rule of faith it is instead concerned to ensure that we preserve belief in the distinction of Persons while adhering to the full unity of God. As a rule, its principal function is to guard against wrong belief, to establish the boundaries of right belief, and to guide the church's language in worship.

Faith Seeking Understanding

Christian doctrines function in a second distinct way—namely, as objects of understanding. As rules of faith, doctrines do not prescribe a certain way of conceiving or imagining Jesus Christ or the Trinity. They employ metaphorical language (such as Father and Son) but do not attempt to give us a theoretical understanding of God. They give us propositions that guard against error but do not prescribe a particular mental picture of God.

At the same time, the Christian tradition has a rich heritage of faithful attempts to gain understanding of God. Such attempts are of course always accompanied by the recognition that God is infinite and transcends human understanding (Rom. 11:33–36). Nonetheless, because God is truth, we are encouraged to explore the truth of God within the limits within which human rationality operates. Seeking to understand is, accordingly, not a quest to satisfy curiosity but is an exercise in worshipful thinking. In such a quest, we offer up our frail, fallible ideas and beliefs to God and trust that God's grace will use them to strengthen our faith and grant coherence to our thoughts.

An early example of faith seeking understanding of the Trinity was the metaphor of the sun with its heat and light. Acknowledging that something physical cannot be a true representation of God, the metaphor nonetheless yields insight in certain ways. It illustrates how one thing (heat or light) can proceed from another thing (the sun), sharing in the nature of that thing, being at once both distinct (heat, light, and the sun are distinct) and yet one in essence. This simple, physical metaphor thus helps us as we think about the generation of the Son and the procession of the Spirit and about how the Trinitarian Persons can be distinct yet one in essence and inseparable.

Augustine offered a more sophisticated set of analogies. One of these has come to have special historical importance: the three mental functions of memory, intellect, and will. (For Augustine, memory is the mind's storehouse of ideas.) This triad of functions subsists in utter unity, since they are functions of one mind. At the same time, these three functions are clearly distinct, each with its own defining property. Memory is not intellect, and intellect is not will; yet none exists except in relation to the others: intellect has nothing to think about without the ideas stored in memory; will cannot desire something unless that thing is first conceived by the intellect. These three functions, then, constitute an analogy of the Trinity. Of course, they are *only* an analogy—a model with which we are familiar and that gives us a way of thinking about the Trinity. It is not as though God is a mind with memory, intellect, and will. But by using this familiar analogy, we are able to think in helpful and creative ways about God, thus avoiding absolute silence.

The history of Trinitarian thought contains another helpful analogy that is sometimes called the "social analogy" because, more than Augustine's triad of mental functions, it emphasizes the Trinity of Persons. This analogy was first proposed by Richard of St. Victor (d. 1173) and is based on the logic of love. In love, three elements can be distinguished: the lover, the object of the love, and the love itself. Augustine had already suggested such an analogy, but Richard gave it a far greater elaboration. The value of this analogy is that, instead of likening God to a mind with three functions, it compares God to persons between whom there is a relation of love. In this way it gives us a more concrete way of depicting the Trinitarian Persons as *hupostaseis*.

None of these analogies, and no other attempt at understanding, constitute the doctrine of the Trinity. That doctrine is enshrined in the statements of the ecumenical creeds. The analogies we have briefly reviewed are simply attempts to gain insight, to think concretely about the God who is above thought, and to avoid the silence that must prevail without the use of metaphors. As such, these analogies are not objects of faith but means of understanding the faith.

The Ethical Function of Christian Doctrine

Christian doctrine exists in the form of words. This fact can mislead us into thinking that doctrine is only or even primarily about cognitive belief. This is a temptation to which many in Christian history have succumbed; it is all too easy to think that Christianity is principally about believing certain things. It is true that Christianity has formulated doctrines that are important, especially as rules of faith. However, it would be a great mistake to reduce Christianity or Christian faith to belief.

It would also be a mistake to think that Christian faith is a matter of adding practice to belief, as though to believe a doctrine is one thing and to have a practice is another thing, or as though we have certain practices because we believe certain things. Thinking in these ways destroys the unity of belief and practice, opening up the possibility of a contradiction between the two or reducing Christian faith to one or the other.

We must accordingly think of Christian faith as having two elements—belief and practice—that should never be separated. Christian faith is practical belief—the sort of belief that is behaviorally embodied; it is faithful practice—not simply practice but practice that is the practice *of* belief.

The unity of belief and practice is suggested by statements in the Gospel and Letters of John that speak of our *doing* the truth (John 3:21; 1 John 1:6; 3:18; 3 John 4). Truth, in the Johannine tradition, is not simply the object of cognitive knowledge; it is something ethical, something we are to perform. This theme is expressed as well in the pastoral epistles, where we find mention of teaching and knowledge that are according to piety (1 Tim. 6:3; Titus 1:1). We learn that the purpose of this teaching is love (1 Tim. 1:3-5) and that there are certain virtues appropriate to healthy teaching (Titus 2:1-10). Finally, Scripture is said to be useful for training in righteousness so that we can be equipped for good works (2 Tim. 3:15-17). These texts show that doctrine is not only or even mainly about cognitive belief but is instead a matter of piety, of love, of virtuous character, and of righteousness. Finally, consider 1 John 4, which states that it is those who love who know God and that whoever does not love does not know God (vv. 7-8). The knowledge of God, in other words, is found in love. It is not that we know God and also practice love; instead we know God *as* we practice love.

We may therefore understand the doctrine of the Trinity not primarily as an object of cognitive belief but as a faith to be practiced—a truth with doctrinal and ethical content. What does it mean to practice this doctrine? We must return to our point of departure: God's Trinitarian life is one of movement, of going out and returning, of going out to that which is not God and uniting with it. It is a life of love and unity in which the Trinitarian Persons live in and through one another. The church is the historical extension of this divine life into the world; it is called to be the earthly actualization of God's Trinitarian life, the community of love and unity. To practice the doctrine of the Trinity is to be incorporated into the Trinitarian community. It is to participate in its mission of inviting the world to see God's love and unity and to join the community of communion. It is to daily participate in God's movement of outgoing love that embraces that which is not God and unites with it. It is to participate in the church's worship, whereby the community participates in the eschatological return of all things to God in fulfilled worship. It is constantly to make all of life a prayer to God the Father, in the name of God the Son, and in the power of God the Holy Spirit.

So we honor the Trinity, and we make God an object of faith not only by acts of cognitive belief but also by living the doctrine—the reality—of the Trinity, by realizing its communal and ethical content in daily practice.

The Doctrine of the Trinity as Prayer

We are called to make all of life a prayer to God; this includes our doctrine. How is that possible? Prayer is an offering to God. Typically, it is words that are offered to God. But prayer is more than spoken words directed to God. Prayer is human words and all of human life offered to God in the name and authority of Jesus and in the power of the Spirit. Consider Paul's words: "In the same way, the Spirit helps us in our weakness. We do not know what we ought to pray for, but the Spirit himself intercedes for us through wordless groans. And he who searches our hearts knows the mind of the Spirit, because the Spirit intercedes for God's people in accordance with the will of God" (Rom. 8:26–27). This passage shows us that prayers are, as mere human works, nearly meaningless. Our words become prayer only as the Holy Spirit takes them and intercedes with God. The Holy Spirit consecrates our words so that they become prayer. Think about what Paul said in 1 Corinthians: "No one can say, 'Jesus is Lord,' except by the Holy Spirit" (12:3). Here, even our confessions of faith are made possible by the Spirit.

If we think of prayer as something offered to God the Father, in the name of Jesus, and in the power of the Spirit, then our doctrines can be prayers. They are not merely human formulations, strings of words intended to say something. They are also the church's attempt to be faithful to the revelation of the Trinitarian God. The church speaks these words and gives them to God. It does so in the name of Jesus, hoping thereby to honor him. It does so in the power of the Holy Spirit, trusting that, as with ordinary prayer, the Spirit will take our words and intercede with God the Father so that they become fit for God and God's purposes.

In the final analysis, then, the doctrine of the Trinity is not a theory but an act of worship, an offering to God. Like our prayers and our sermons and everything else, we give it to God in gratitude for God's grace and trust that God will make our words acts of worship.

In view of these things, let us close this book with Paul's Trinitarian doxology found in 2 Corinthians 13:14: *"May the grace of the Lord Jesus Christ, and the love of God, and the fellowship of the Holy Spirit be with you all."* Amen.

Suggestions for Further Reading

Kelly, J. N. D. *Early Christian Creeds.* 3rd ed. London; New York: Continuum, 2006.

Norris, Richard A. *The Christological Controversy.* Sources of Early Christian Thought. Philadelphia: Fortress Press, 1980.

Powell, Samuel M. *Discovering Our Christian Faith: An Introduction to Theology.* Kansas City, MO: Beacon Hill Press of Kansas City, 2008.

Rusch, William G. *The Trinitarian Controversy.* Sources of Early Christian Thought. Philadelphia: Fortress Press, 1980.

Young, Frances M. *From Nicaea to Chalcedon: A Guide to the Literature and Its Background.* Philadelphia: Fortress Press, 2010.

Glossary

Adoptionistic Christology: A view of Christ according to which Jesus was a human being who, at his baptism, received divinity as the Old Testament prophets received the Spirit. It has no place for a full union of divine and human natures.

Christology: The church's doctrine about Jesus Christ, especially with respect to the unity of his person and his divine and human natures.

Deification: The process by which human beings come to imitate God and share in God's nature. This is the Latin-based equivalent of the Greek term *theosis*.

Docetism: A view of Christ according to which Christ did not have a real body and therefore did not truly suffer and die but only *appeared* to suffer and die. This view is most clearly associated with the second century writer Marcion.

Double procession of the Spirit: The affirmation, common among churches in the West, that the Holy Spirit proceeds from the Father and the Son, in contrast to the view prevalent in the East that the Spirit proceeds only from the Father.

Ecclesiology: The church's doctrine about the church.

Economic Trinity: The Trinity as it enters into human history in acts of creation, redemption, and sanctification.

Ecumenical Council: A council that has come to be regarded as representative of the entire church and whose results accordingly have greater authority than those of other councils. The ancient Trinitarian and christological creeds (Nicean, Constantinopolitan, and Chalcedonian) were created by ecumenical councils.

Election: The idea that God has chosen Israel and then the church as the holy people of God.

Eschatology: The church's doctrine relating to "last things," such as judgment, resurrection, and the return of Christ.

Essential Trinity: The Trinity in its eternal being. A synonym of "ontological Trinity."

Filioque: A Latin word that means "and from the Son." It was added to the creed of Constantinople by churches in the West and became the occasion for a longstanding controversy between those churches and the churches of the East.

General Revelation: The revelation of God that is available to everyone, regardless of historical circumstances. The natural world is usually regarded as the main source of general revelation.

Homoousios: Of one substance, being, or essence. This term appears in the creeds of Nicea and Constantinople to indicate the unity of the Father and the Son.

Hypostatic Union: A term that denotes the union of Christ's person: Jesus Christ is a single, divine-human *hupostasis*, not two distinct *hupostaseis*, one divine and the other human.

Immutability: That property whereby God does not and cannot change.

Impassibility: That property whereby God does not and cannot suffer.

Incarnation: The event in which the divine *logos* is united with human flesh, thus constituting the human being Jesus Christ.

Justification: God's act of putting us in the right, of making us righteous before the law.

Koinonia: A Greek term that means fellowship or communion.

Logos: A Greek word with numerous meanings, including reason, thought, mind, spoken word, and proportion. In theological discourse it refers to God's Word, the second Person of the Trinity.

Macedonians: An early Christian group that accepted the divinity of the Son but not the divinity of the Spirit. Their view was rejected at the Council of Constantinople.

Mission: In Trinitarian discourse, "mission" refers to the Father's sending of the Son and then the Holy Spirit into the world. The missions into the world parallel the eternal processions of the Son and the Spirit from the Father.

Modalism: An early Christian view of the Trinity that denied the distinctness of the Trinitarian Persons. In one version of modalism, the persons are simply different names of the one God, different modes of appearing to creatures.

Monarchy: The unity of God, in contrast to the distinction of the Trinitarian persons.

Monogenes: A Greek term understood by early Christian writers to be a reference to the Son's being generated by the Father.

Monotheism: Belief in one God.

Natural Theology: The view that some knowledge of God is possible through the exercise of common human reason.

Oikonomia: A Greek term whose common meaning is "management" or "administration." Tertullian used *dispensatio* to translate *oikonomia* and to indicate the arrangement of the Trinitarian Persons within God's being. It is also used to indicate God's activity in human salvation.

Ontological Trinity: Another term for the Trinity in its eternal being. See "Essential Trinity."

Perichoresis: A Greek term sometimes used to portray the unity of the Trinitarian Persons by means of the metaphor of a Greek dancing chorus.

Pneumatology: The church's doctrine of the Holy Spirit.

Possession Christology: A view of Christ according to which Jesus received divinity at his baptism, comparable to the way in which the Old Testament prophets received the Holy Spirit.

Regeneration: Another term for the new birth, an aspect of salvation.

Sanctification: The process by which Christian disciples become like God and participate in God's nature.

Soteriology: The Christian doctrine of salvation.

Telos: A Greek term that designates a goal or purpose.

Theosis: A Greek term equivalent to deification—the process of becoming like God and sharing in God's nature.

Theotokos: The Virgin Mary, described as the "God bearer."

Word-flesh Christology: The Christology according to which Jesus Christ was the divine *logos* united with human flesh but lacking a human mind.